Personal Narrative Performance and Storytelling

Personal Narrative Performance and Storytelling: A Method of Composition from Action to Text offers a practical method for composing and performing personal narrative stories for artistic and academic purposes.

It is designed to make storytelling accessible to seasoned performers and people who are engaging with the artform for the first time. The author's unique method of composing stories from action to text privileges oral composition over writing. It draws on anecdotes from the author's many years of coaching storytellers to illustrate concepts throughout the book, making it entertaining and user-friendly. The methods contained in this book can help students and scholars communicate theoretical and scholarly arguments about culture, gender, race, and the environment.

Anyone looking to harness the power of personal storytelling to speak about the political and the personal—in a classroom or on a stage—will find *Personal Narrative Performance and Storytelling: A Method of Composition from Action to Text* of great use. Additionally, the book will be of interest to qualitative researchers and those applying autoethnographic and storytelling methods in communication studies and other related social science and arts disciplines.

Charles Parrott is an Associate Professor in the Department of Theatre & Performance Studies at Kennesaw State University, USA. Dr. Parrott is the Director of the KSU Tellers, a student storytelling ensemble focused on solo performance, community engagement, and performance-based scholarship. Under his direction, the KSU Tellers have performed at regional, national, and international festivals and conferences. He has won numerous awards for his innovative teaching and mentorship of undergraduate research.

Personal Narrative Performance and Storytelling

A Method of Composition from Action to Text

Charles Parrott

LONDON AND NEW YORK

Designed cover image: Normform / Getty Images

First published 2024
by Routledge
4 Park Square, Milton Park, Abingdon, Oxon OX14 4RN

and by Routledge
605 Third Avenue, New York, NY 10158

Routledge is an imprint of the Taylor & Francis Group, an informa business

British Library Cataloguing-in-Publication Data
A catalogue record for this book is available from the British Library

ISBN: 978-0-367-48313-5 (hbk)
ISBN: 978-0-367-48314-2 (pbk)
ISBN: 978-1-003-03926-6 (ebk)

DOI: 10.4324/9781003039266

Typeset in Optima
by KnowledgeWorks Global Ltd.

This book is dedicated to the students who participated in TPS 4010 Storytelling Practicum for the past 12 years. Not all of you appear in this book but each of you has left an indelible mark on me as a teacher, as a storyteller, and as a person. Your commitment, creativity, and your stories are what made this book possible. I thank you for all you've given me, and I hope that you enjoy the book.

Contents

Acknowledgments

Though writing can certainly feel like a solitary endeavor, all books require many helping hands to come to fruition. First, I want to acknowledge my home institution, Kennesaw State University, for supporting this project at various points and in various ways. There is so much to love about KSU and I am thankful for all it has done for me. I am grateful to my colleagues Chuck Meacham and Esther Jordan who graciously took the time to help keep me on task. I must also thank Jess Maillet, my research assistant, whose careful contributions helped to get this book across the finish line. Finally, I thank my wife, family, friends, and colleagues who patiently supported me during this process.

Introduction

I don't usually talk to strangers on airplanes, but I needed to talk to somebody. It was nighttime, I was tired. I was returning home after spending two days interviewing for my first job since coming to the end of my PhD program. The genial older woman sitting next to me on the plane was happy to listen as I tried to make sense of things. The job was in a department of theatre and performance studies. My PhD was in Speech Communication, and I was focused on performance studies, but I was no expert on theatre. They wanted me to teach, among other things, storytelling. The genial older woman asked me what that was. I told her … I wasn't really sure. It could mean a lot of things, but they had a storytelling troupe and they wanted someone to direct it and they wanted that person to do it well. The interview went well, I thought there was a good chance that they wanted me. I was not sure what I would do if I got the job. She left me with some version of, "I'm sure you'll figure it out" and we went our separate ways. A few days later I was offered the job.

I did not know how to teach storytelling when I started my career, but it felt like my life depended on my ability to figure it out. Luckily, dozens and dozens of students came along over the next 12 years, and *they* taught me how to teach storytelling. They brought me ideas and we nurtured them together. They brought me problems and we solved them together. I wanted to do a good job for them because I genuinely liked them. Together we've created nearly 100 outward-facing performance events and hundreds of different stories. The program, known as the KSU Tellers—in reference to the institution that gave me the job, Kennesaw State University—has become a hallmark of our university and they are known far and wide for their outstanding work. It turns out that lady on the plane was right, I did figure it out. But I needed my students to make it happen.

My goal is always to get audiences to see my students and their stories the way I see them—as something magical. Perhaps it is because storytelling is such a magic trick—starting with nothing and conjuring something right in front of the eyes of the audience. Maybe the magic is the emotional roller coaster ride that a good storyteller can create. Maybe college students are just bursting with motion because they are changing so rapidly and maybe there is magic in that. Maybe it is not magic at all. Maybe it is just a matter of hormones being released when you laugh, when you empathize, and when you witness someone standing up and saying what they feel. I'm not always prone to optimism but time has taught me that everyone has something interesting to say. And I have learned that when someone stands up and commands a room with a great story, they can transcend the everyday world and reach something beyond it. The undefinable thing that happens when an audience and a storyteller are in sync is truly nothing short of magical.

This book is designed with students and teachers in mind, though I hesitate to call it a textbook. It is not meant to be a comprehensive look at storytelling but, rather, a very specific description of a method of composing personal stories to be performed live in front of an audience. In my research, I've discovered several lovely books designed for a popular audience (rather than an academic one) that offer guidance in creating personal stories. There is also a large corpus of scholarship about personal storytelling in the academic world. But I have yet to come across a book that tries to bridge the gap between these two worlds by offering an academic look at the practical business of personal storytelling, and that is a shame. It is a shame because I know that performance and storytelling are "having a moment" in popular culture and in academic circles. Solo performers are taking the stage on Broadway, comedians are blurring the lines between standup and storytelling, and storytelling podcasts continue to grow in popularity. Across the country, teachers are asking students to use personal narrative storytelling as an entry point to talk about healthcare, racism, the environment, and every other important topic of the day. It may seem like talking about yourself and your experience should be easy, but it is actually an artform just like any other. This is my effort to step in between popular storytelling guides and academic tomes to offer a book rooted in the marriage of theory and practice.

I have been teaching for a long time and every time I ask my students to read something, I ask them how they feel about what they read. Sometimes they like it, sometimes they don't. But the time and again their responses tell me this: they want to read a book that is clear and useful. I hear and respect that position, so I have tried to make this book clear and useful in a few different ways.

First, I have made every effort to make this book sound conversational. I hope that it feels to you like we're chatting about stories in my office or like I'm coaching you in-person in a classroom where we both are comfortable. I have deliberately avoided trying to sound too "academic" (although sometimes I just can't help myself) in favor of prose that meets readers where they are. I always have the most success coaching stories through conversation. I have a feeling that having a relationship with my students aids me in helping them with their stories. Sadly, that kind of relationship is not something that we can easily scale up. I can't visit all your classes, all your homes, and have a chat. I think that writing in a conversational style is the next best thing.

Second, I have tried to be as concise as possible. One of the things that I love about storytelling is that it is a moving target. It will not sit still and be just one thing. It can manifest in many different ways, even when we narrow the medium to telling personal stories on stage. Because storytelling is so multi-faceted one could go on and on trying to capture every nuance and detail. But that would make for a dense, and therefore less useful, book. Instead, I have tried to get to the most important parts of each chapter while leaving out anything that feels superfluous. Stories that are specific are often the most vivid. It is my sincere hope that keeping this book concise will make my ideas more visible to you as a reader.

Third, this book is full of tools, not rules. Rules are hard and fast and you should not break them. Tools can be used however you like. You can use a screwdriver to open a paint can. You can use a corkscrew to drill a hole in your wall. You can fill a bucket with water, or you can flip it over and use it as a stool. It is not so important that you use a tool correctly. What is important is that it works. I'm going to give you all sorts of guidance in this book but it is up to you to figure out how to make it work for you. That means more work for you but it also means that what you learn will mean more to you when you're done. I think this approach makes this book more useful than a book full of rules.

Finally, in order to make this book clear and useful I have populated it with the stories of my former students, students who were probably a lot like you. While you read this book, you'll meet person after person that I have worked with. You'll learn what they learned about storytelling and what I learned from them. Having them appear in this book makes it feel as if they were right alongside me as I wrote each chapter and that was a great comfort.

These students were talented, but they were still just normal people. Each of them was just like you. They were nervous sometimes. They were frustrated sometimes. They didn't know where to start. But, just like you, they were people with something to say who needed to figure out how to say it. So, just as they were my companions as I wrote this book, they can be your companions as you read it. Teaching these ideas through the stories my students told is meant to make this book feel relatable and fun to read.

Each chapter of this book includes a transcript of a story mentioned in the chapter. We used videos of the stories to capture the text. I mention that these are transcripts to remind you that, for the most part, this is not a book about writing stories. It is a book about composing stories. These stories all came to life on stage, not on the page. At the end of each chapter you'll find a set of questions and prompts to help you keep going on your storytelling journey. But, in the end, it will be up to you to stand up and start working on your story. Know this: you already have everything inside you that you need to be successful at storytelling. This book is just meant to show you the way.

1 "Why We Leave Home": Defining Personal Storytelling

I'd like to take responsibility for Tori and her skill as a storyteller, but, honestly, she was a natural. Maybe that's not the best thing to tell you at the start of this book—that some people just have a knack for doing the thing you bought a book to learn how to do—but sometimes there are people like Tori. I worked with Tori on several stories, but my favorite one was called *Why We Leave Home*. Tori was raised to be careful and fearful of strangers and danger, but when she visited Dublin, Ireland, to study, her hesitance about unfamiliar things was tested. After many days in Dublin, Tori's friends prevailed on her to explore the city's nightlife and pub culture. Her story unfolded hilariously as she cautiously projects her drink, deals with the noise and smoke of pubs, and fends off hapless and harmless Irish boys looking to impress her and her friends. This kind of night with friends, with excitement, and new experiences, *this is why we leave home*. No sooner does she come to this conclusion than a stranger lurking on the Dublin streets does become aggressive and, just like that, Tori is afraid once again. But she stays safe, and winds up changed for the better, no longer so afraid of leaving home.

Tori's story taught me a lot. Her comedic timing, her turns of phrase, her self-aware impersonation of her own anxiety—it all stands out as exceptional. But Tori's story can also act as a metaphor for the experience of crafting and telling stories on stage. We are taught that sharing too much can be fraught with danger, that "putting yourself out there" can leave you humiliated. But if we take a leap of faith, as Tori did in Dublin, there are beautiful things (and a few scary ones) out there waiting for us.

Storytelling is the art of getting a group of people to see, think, and feel the same thing at the same time. The mediums of storytelling vary—from journalism to blockbuster movies, to novels, to the spoken word around a campfire. Some stories are true, some are fantasy, some are outright lies. Each medium of storytelling has its own benefits and drawbacks. However, in their most central intention, all storytellers attempt to do the same thing: give their audience an imaginative, intellectual, and emotional experience that they can share.

In this book, we're going to narrow our conversation about storytelling to focus on the particular medium of personal narrative storytelling, or stories

DOI: 10.4324/9781003039266-1

we tell about ourselves. Personal narrative storytelling orders real events from your life into a narrative structure that can easily be shared with others. In this way, personal narrative storytelling is an excellent way to narrate and stage episodes that illustrate the human condition. Along the way, personal narrative storytellers almost always take some time to comment on the action and reflect on the events they are narrating. The ability to step out of a story, and comment on the action, makes personal narrative storytelling an excellent way to critically reflect on human behavior and the culture where it takes place. All of this narration and reflection is delivered through carefully chosen language and embodiment, making personal narrative storytelling a charming delivery system for cultural analysis and personal reflection.

This chapter lays down some foundational concepts to help us understand what is going on when we tell stories. We'll discuss storytelling as communication and storytelling as performance. Next, we will bring communication and performance together to see how they become identifiable as personal narrative storytelling.

Storytelling as Communication

It's easy to think of communication as the mere relay of a message, across a medium, between one person and another. This definition conjures up the image of two people engaging in the very practical business of talking on the telephone. In fact, for a long time, the telephone model of communication held a dominant place in conversations about communication. To some extent, that model offers insight by at least identifying some of the relevant features in play in most (if not all) communication contexts. It includes a sender, a receiver, a message, and a medium—the phone line—which are all part of pretty much all behaviors that we would label "communication." However, this technically minded definition leaves out the social and emotional dimensions that are so central to communication.

John Durham Peters offers my favorite definition of communication as "an apparent answer to the painful divisions between self and other, private and public, and inner thought and outer word; the notion illustrates our strange lives at this point in history" (2). Some dark part of me relates to the feeling that human beings are condemned to spend our lives as islands, desperately reaching out to one another but never being fully understood. I like the idea of communication as the answer or remedy to this fundamental problem of existence—our distance from one another—rather than an object or technical procedure. Sometimes it's useful to view communication as a technical procedure, like when you're giving someone driving directions or telling them how to set up their new computer. But all too often, when we see communication as a technical procedure, we forget that real bodies, emotions, experiences, and possibilities are involved. Telling personal stories can help to bring the body, with all its complex senses and emotions, back into the conversation about what communication can and should mean.

A person telling a story, their story, is a moment charged with meaning. In that moment, another person becomes more fully real to us. All mediums of communication—written texts, carefully staged movies and television, videos of something that happened days before—mediate the body of the person sending the message. While the medium is necessary to convey the message—through text, video, and so on—it also stands between the sender and receiver. It is almost as if the sender is wrapped in a puffy coat that blocks the receiver's ability to reach the sender. A storyteller on stage materializes their body in front of the bodies of a live audience. The puffy coat of mediation is removed. The audience imagines the sensations described by the storyteller. They don't just receive a message; they feel the emotions evoked by the storyteller. In this way, personal storytelling brings all the complexity of emotion and affect back into the conversation about communication.

On a more philosophical level, the storyteller standing alone on stage and telling her story implicitly brings forth the particularity of her experience. Sometimes, it seems that much of the world values science and objective facts over everything else. Sometimes it seems that the only way one can "prove" something is "true" is to provide empirical data. Science is important and empirical data is valuable. I wouldn't want someone to tell me how they *feel* about building a bridge or designing an airplane. I want to see the plans and make sure they check the math. Because objective truth and empirical data are so important, we sometimes come to think they are all that is important. Storytelling values the knowledge of grandmothers on porches, dads at kitchen tables, teenagers who've felt heartbreak, women who've given birth, and everyone who's made a winning shot at the buzzer. All the human drama we experience, in and through our bodies, gives us a theory of knowledge that allows us to make claims about what is true. Storytellers communicate all this human drama through an aesthetic mode of communication we call performance.

Storytelling as Performance

To say that personal narrative storytelling "dramatizes experience" is to say that it turns experience into performance. Performance is a tough term to define. There is disagreement about what counts as performance. It encompasses a broad range of behaviors, ranging from Shakespearean actors to standup comedians to buskers on street corners. There are academic disciplinary boundaries between fields like theatre, communication, and fine art where the term may mean very different things. Further complicating matters, practically all human behavior can be understood *as* performance. In other words, we can understand everyday behaviors as performances that constitute identity and signify meaning. Something as simple as taking a shower in the morning can be viewed as a ritual performance of grooming, a ritual we engage in out of a desire to meet social expectations—like hygiene—which are also produced by other performances, such as social cues, by people around us who don't want us to smell. We perform other social rituals, like tailgating at a football game. Those events include special foods, special clothes, and chants and songs to support the team. When you think about it, that sort of social performance is not so different from a more formal ritual ceremony, like a wedding. Most weddings also feature special foods, special clothes, and many include songs and the recitation of special words. As you can see, it's not hard to see most human behavior *as* performance.

While we're at it, let's add another layer of complexity and take note of the fact that many (if not most) personal narrative stories dramatize events that were performances to begin with. Plenty of stories center on rituals like birthday parties, the observance of religious or national holidays, and coming-of-age events like graduations. All those things can be easily understood as performance. In fact, when you start looking at the world through the lens of performance, it can be hard to see what isn't easily understood as performance. So, some performances are performances about performances. When everything can be viewed *as* performance, it can be easy to lose sight of what performance is.

While the whole field of study that looks at human behavior as performance is very valuable, we will be discussing performance of a less subtle kind. When we say "performance," we will be talking about performance that is conspicuously staged and intentionally meant to be understood as performance. Tracy Stephenson Shaffer defines conspicuously staged performance, "as a distinct, rehearsed, and staged performance, marked as art through stylistic choices and set apart from everyday life by meta-communicative frames" (1). The most unfamiliar part of this definition is the last part, performance setting itself apart from everyday life by a "meta-communicative frame." A metacommunicative frame refers to the way the context of a performance frames it as a performance. A Broadway musical on a stage, a stand-up comedian in a nightclub, or a singer busking for change on a street corner are all examples of performances that are defined, in part, by the context in which they occur. In the case of personal narrative storytelling, you'll rehearse the use of stylistic choices to ultimately do a performance in a space marked for performance, whether it is standing on a stage or in a classroom, or in front of a podcast microphone, or in any of the other settings we tell stories.

Despite the fact that there is so much uncertainty around the definition of performance, there are some characteristics that help it take shape. Richard Bauman (1977), a folklorist quite interested in storytelling, argued that there are three constitutive elements of performance: performance competence, audience evaluation, and heightened experience. For Bauman, performance competence refers to the ability to speak and behave in ways that are appropriate to the situation. This not only refers to knowing what to say but also knowing how to say it. Gesture, posture, timing, and vocal quality are just a few of the ways we assess performance competency beyond simply knowing what to say. In storytelling, we can refer to the things a storyteller says as the content dimension of the story. We can refer to things like facial expressions or tone of voice as part of the affective dimension of storytelling. Affective displays are nonverbal communication that help color and shape the meaning of what is being said. Throughout this book, we'll talk about ways to align the content dimension of your storytelling with the affective dimension of your performance to maximize your performance competence.

Performance competence is usually assessed by an audience, which leads to Bauman's second constitutive element of performance: audience evaluation. Almost every conspicuously staged performance is staged for other people to see. Those "other people" are the audience, and they create a dynamic interplay with the performer. They respond with approval or disapproval, using a range of behaviors—from polite applause to storming the stage—to communicate their feelings. Sometimes audience evaluation comes after the fact, when audience members tell their friends about a performance, or follow the performer on social media, or buy another ticket to see the show again. Beyond these sorts of obvious responses, the relationship between an audience and a performer can, under the best circumstances, produce a magical feeling of shared connection. At the start of this chapter, I asserted that storytelling is the art of getting a group of people to see, think, and feel the same thing at the same time. That group of people is composed of the audience and performer having a shared experience together. When it works, the audience leaves feeling as if they have all shared something special. We'll talk about your relationship with the audience at greater length in Chapter 8.

Finally, Bauman argues that we know something is a conspicuous and intentional performance when it is part of a heightened experience. That phrase, "heightened experience," refers to an event that feels set off from everyday life, an event where something special is happening. No one attends a concert by accident. You purchase tickets, decide what to wear, travel to the venue and park, and enter a theater or arena to find your seat. The lights go down, people cheer, music pours forth, and the lights flash—something special is going on. The presence of a stage, which literally elevates one person or a group of people over the audience, is also a common sign that a heightened experience is about to occur. In short, the heightened experience of a performance event separates the performance event from the mundane and the everyday.

Storytelling as Personal Narrative

Personal narrative storytelling is both communication and performance. Communication seeks to close the gap between ourselves and others. Performance is a rehearsed, aesthetic, and conspicuous attempt to close that gap. Personal narrative storytellers try to close that gap by staging their experiences in narrative form. Again, that may seem straight-forward, but I assure, if you scratch just below the surface of "experience," you'll find it is anything but simple. Several entire academic industries are founded on exploring the notion of experience. In the simplest terms, you experience the world through the access points of your body and its senses. That sensory input is filtered through your history, psychology, and interpretive frameworks. Your personal combination of sensory experience and interpretation is uniquely yours. No one experiences the world just like you, so no one has a story just like yours. However, it's likely that you and your audience will share many commonalities of experience. You all have bodies, you all have emotions, you all have desires, and you all have fears. Hearing a familiar story given voice on stage can make both the audience and the teller feel less alone. In what follows, we will spend some time thinking about the form and content of personal narrative storytelling.

Personal narrative storytelling is not a style of performance that is easy to categorize. It is what I consider a nomadic genre (Ben Driss) that crosses the boundaries between generic categories. It doesn't feel or look like one singular, recognizable thing. Linda Park-Fuller points out that the genre-breaking style is "Not exactly like a conventional play, a public speech, a literary narrative, or an autobiographical essay," but "this form, which takes from each, defies traditional identification, containment, and criticism" (22). For the most part, personal narrative storytellers engage in monologue with a minimum of staging and props. Each individual storyteller must decide for themselves in which direction they want to lean, so to speak, with their performances. Some personal narratives feel more like stand-up comedy, some feel more like a stage play, while still others feel more intimate and confessional. I like to think of the form of personal narrative storytelling as an extended, one-sided conversation with an audience. To me, this conception of the form underscores the ways storytellers work to break down the barriers between them and their audience to make an authentic connection. Like the term "performance" itself, the style of personal narrative performance won't sit still. All of this ambiguity can be frustrating, particularly for students who feel most secure when ideas stay comfortably in their boxes. But I assure you, the dynamic motion of performance is a good thing. I like to imagine this constant motion like water turning a turbine, creating power we can put to use.

The content of personal narrative storytelling is your experience. Performance scholar Julie-Ann Scott argues that "stories begin in our viscera; we feel our encounters with others in our stomachs—the quivers of hope, the pangs of embarrassment, the punch of failure"—long before we process those feelings and perform them (119). When we structure and stage our experience, storyteller Margo Leitman defines storytelling as simply "recounting true experience from your life that has a beginning, middle, and an end" (xxv). The experiences we stage can be big or small. In the book *How to Tell a Story*, published by the people who produce live storytelling events called The Moth, the authors explain:

> Some stories take a sweeping episode of history and break moments or interactions down into smaller, more intimate scenes. Others take what might seem like an ordinary event … and imbue it with all the magic you felt in that first moment.
>
> (Bowles, Burns, Hixon, Jenness, and Tellers, 10)

Our experience of the world is always highly subjective, rooted in our own particular point of view. The act of sharing that experience brings other people closer to your point of view, helping them to see the world through your eyes. Seeking that connection is at the heart of personal narrative story-telling. In Chapter 2, we'll discuss some of the reasons or motivations people have for seeking out that connection.

Questions to Consider

1 What performances have you witnessed that moved you emotionally? Create a list of reasons why you were moved by those performances.
2 What are your favorite themes in stories you've heard? Revenge, overcoming challenges, and learning from a mistake are just a few common themes.
3 Read Tori Thompson's story that follows these questions. Create a list of all the ways you notice Tori makes her story a heightened experience for the audience.

"Why We Leave Home"
Created and Performed by Tori Thompson

Don't talk to strangers. Now, I'm not telling you this to scare you, but to remind you that there are mean people in the world. My mother would tell me this all the time and let's just say I took it to heart. By the time I was 20, I had a whole laundry list of rules I invented to keep me safe. Don't go out at night. Don't go out alone. Maybe most days don't go out at all. Dress modestly so as to avoid unwanted attention. Stand up straight *[stands straight]* so you look like you know what you're doing. And above all, do not talk to strangers. There are mean people in the world. *[Looks all around]*

As you can imagine, this made it difficult for me to ever leave my comfort zone. When I told my parents that I wanted to go study acting for the summer in Ireland, they were like, "Yes?" *[With shocked face]* Which really means like, "We're skeptical of this, and that sounds expensive," but they helped me go. When I got to Dublin, I couldn't believe how perfect this place was for me.

I was there with two other girls in the program. Some of you may know them, Kimberly, and Amy. But for those of you who don't, Kimberly is this super friendly Jimmy Fallon fanatic, and Amy is this sarcastic baker with the voice of an angel. We were like a sitcom dream team! Spent all our time together going to museums that were hyper educational. Seeing more theater in one week in Dublin than we did in three months in Kennesaw. And then we would window shop the antique stores. You guys, Irish antiques make American antiques look like jelly bracelets from the early 2000s. Just saying. *[Puts hands up]*

There was this whole other part of Dublin that we hadn't looked into yet—Nightlife. *[Raises eyebrows]* So far, my idea of nightlife was getting an ice cream cone past 5:00 PM. But when Hannah came to town, that all changed.

Now some of you may also know Hannah, she was a graduate of KSU. She also went to the Irish summer acting program, and then last summer she moved to Ireland, because when you're an adult, you can make those kinds of decisions. *[Claps hands]* You go girl.

Hannah is what I would describe as, a lot. A lot of cool clothes, and a lot of big hair, and a lot of personality, and a hell of a lot of a good time. Sorry for swearing. But she was going to be the one to take us on our first Irish night out. We started at a pub near the hostel called The Grand Social, which sounds very posh, but was really what I imagine most bars in America look like. Dark, smoky, *[Raises voice]* needlessly loud. The girls ordered their drinks. And there's something you guys should know about me. I don't drink, like at all, and in a foreign country doesn't seem like the best place to start, but you guys, I was in Ireland, land of Guinness and Jameson, and I would feel so awkward going up to this bartender, and being all like, "Can I get a water with lemon please?"

So I don't. I get a Bulmers, which is a cider, which is good, because I think ciders are supposed to have a lower alcohol content than other beverages? And this is good, because the bartender hands me a cider, which is huge. *[Motions like holding giant cup with two hands.]* We walk upstairs *[Pretends to walk upstairs]* where everybody's watching a football match, very European. We sit our drinks down at a communal table. *[Puts down giant imaginary cup]* We're flanked by strangers on either side. I cover my drink with my hands, *[Covers giant drink with both hands]* just in case a wee Irish roofie is flying through the air. *[Motions to the air]*

I was more than a little nervous, but I still had a great time. We sat and talked about Ireland, *[Sips giant cup]* and theater, *[Sips from cup again]* and what it really means to be a woman in the world. *[Gulps to drink last of cup]* And after two hours, I had done it! My first Irish pint, my first drink ever, mind you, and nothing bad had happened to me. I couldn't wait to go back to the hostel, and journal about it. I was reaching for my purse, but then Hannah was all like, "You guys want to go to Workman's?" No, we did the thing, whatever that is, I don't want to do it.

But Kimberly, and Amy were like, "What's that?" And of course Hannah was like, "Well, Workman's is like this night club music venue owned by U2." I definitely don't want to do that. But Kimberly, and Amy were all like, "That sounds like fun." And they all looked at me like, "Is that okay, mom?" And I was like, "Ah, yes?" Which of course means no. I don't want to go to a nightclub music venue owned by rock stars. Rock stars are notorious for alcohol poisoning, drug abuse, and sex stuff that is so weird the bluest of comedians probably hasn't heard of it.

But we went. We crossed the River Liffey, and got into Workman's, which at first looks a lot like The Grand Social. It's dark, smokey, *[raises voice]* needlessly loud. The girls order their drinks, and this time I do get a water with lemon, just to start, don't worry. Which is good, because when we get into the next room, everything is so bright and yellow, and in motion. *[Pauses with eyebrows raised]* "Oh my God, I'm tipsy." For the first time in my life, I am drunk off my rocker in a den of sin in a foreign country. This is not what we call safety, folks.

And as I'm coming to this realization, two men in Hawaiian shirts approach our group. "Of course," I think, and I cover my water with my hands. I cannot hear a word these Hawaiian shirts are saying, but I can't imagine it makes much of a difference. They probably just want to dance, and just so you know, dancing is not about dancing anymore, now it's all about sex. I did not want to have sex with these gentlemen. *[Starts to talk in voice that sounds tipsy]*

Whatever happened to the mashed potatoe? Whatever happened to the pony? *[Does dance move]* Now it's all pelvis and chest, *[Dances shaking hips and shaking shoulders]* pelvis and chest. And as I'm thinking about this, I hear one of the Hawaiian shirts say, *[In Irish accent]* "Well, this one's not impressed." I have clearly missed something. And so Amy yells in my ear, *[Shouting]* "They're doing a magic trick." *[Yells back]* "Okay, Sorry, I'm hard of hearing."

"Name a celebrity."

"Dawn French."

"Who's Dawn French?"

"Who's Don French? Some people know her as the fat lady in *Harry Potter and the Prisoner of Azkaban*, others know her as half a British comedy jewel, French and Saunders, but the most important people know her as I know her, the star of my favorite British TV sitcom, *The Vicar of Dibley*. That who Dawn French is you fool."

And we met eyes, and we had an understanding, so he did another magic trick, and he disappeared. *[Waves hand around]* It was at that point in the evening that Amy looked over to me and said something along the lines of, "You don't look so good, Tori." And so I responded something like, *[In drunk voice]* "I don't feel so good, Amy. We should go home."

So we did, we thanked Kimberly and Hannah for a wonderful evening, and we left Workman. Outside in Dublin at night, I suddenly wasn't afraid anymore. All of a sudden, I realized why people do this. Why people take risks, and get drunk in foreign countries, and why we leave home. Everything was so beautiful here. Amy's face was so beautiful. The River Liffey at night was so beautiful. The people rushing in and out of pubs, the nighttime man who was walking toward us, he said, *[In Irish accent]* "Good evening ladies."

What a nice nighttime, man. *[With hands on hips]* "Good evening, sir."

"Oh, you're American. What are you doing in Dublin?"

"We're studying acting. Thank you for your interest."

"Oh, you're actresses, show me your angry face." And he started walking toward me, and so he wouldn't get the wrong idea, I took a couple of steps back. But he kept coming forward, and he said, "Show me your sexy face."

And just like that, I was afraid again. And he started to reach out for me. *[Holds hands out]* But then somebody across the street grabbed his hand, *[Grabs one arm with the other]* and pulled him in the other direction.

I grabbed Amy, and he rushed back to the hostel, and when we got back, what could I do? I got undressed. I put on my pajamas. Climbed to the top bunk and put my head on the pillow. Mom was right. There are mean people in the world. But you know what? There are good people, too. There's that mysterious person who grabbed the man from across the street. There's Amy, who made sure I was okay and fed me McVitie's double chocolate biscuits in bed. Kimberly and Hannah made sure I had a really nice time. And of course, there's my parents, and without them, I wouldn't be here. Not just like here in Dublin, but existing in the universe. And then there's Dawn French. *[Looks up]* Thank you God for Dawn French.

2 "I Didn't Learn Anything": Motivations for Telling Stories on Stage

Daniel came to me with a story about the night he and his friends got drunk and broke into their high school to impress some girls. They were, not surprisingly, caught on security cameras, hauled into the school principal's office, and suspended from school. It's the kind of story that doesn't need much embellishment to be exciting and funny. Daniel thought it was a slam dunk idea, except for one thing: we couldn't agree on what the story was *about*. I asked Daniel, "did you learn some important lesson from this experience?" Surely, I thought, this adventure had taught him to be more careful and less reckless. He shook his head, "no, I didn't learn anything. I don't regret it at all." I paused, "well," I said to Daniel, "I don't think you want to get up in front of people and tell a story about getting drunk and trespassing." He was undeterred. "No," he smiled, "I'm pretty sure that I do." If I was going to help Daniel with his story, I needed to believe that the story was about something meaningful. I was sure it was about something meaningful. I just didn't know what it was yet. I was not yet thinking about all the possible reasons we might tell stories.

This chapter is about identifying some of the motivations for telling stories on stage. There are, of course, any number of reasons to tell stories about your experience, but here we will focus on three: personal motives for storytelling, ideological motives for storytelling, and academic motives for storytelling. These are not discrete categories. Any single story might serve all these motives, but we will examine them individually so they get the attention they deserve.

Personal Motives for Storytelling

Quite a few years ago, one of my students observed that "storytelling can be therapeutic, but it isn't therapy." This quip goes a long way toward encapsulating the personal motives one might have for telling personal stories on stage. It's not fair to dump your feelings on an audience, as one would a therapist, and storytelling is certainly no substitute for therapy. Therapy is the excavation and examination of experience and emotion, with an eye toward improving one's wellbeing. Storytelling carefully structures experience

DOI: 10.4324/9781003039266-2

and emotion into a product designed for an audience. Far too many people confuse the need for an emotional outlet with a desire to perform. But the process of developing a story can offer insight into our own lived experiences. Telling stories about yourself can help you make sense of your past, understand the present, and imagine the future. Furthermore, telling stories about yourself can offer a sense of pleasure and edification that is unique to the medium.

Telling stories about yourself can be an effective way to make sense of your memories of the past and take ownership over them. I do not think I am the only person who looks at their past and says, "what the heck happened back there? What did it mean? Why did I behave that way? How did it affect me?" We may remember what happened, but we may not understand what it means. Memories, particularly difficult ones, seem to hold a kind of power over us, as if they are some external forces imposed on us by the past. As if they don't belong to us at all. Whether you just got very embarrassed one day in middle school or suffered genuine abuse, the experience of trauma in particular can grab ahold of us and not let go. The process of composing personal narrative performances requires that you order and articulate the events of the past. In doing so, the storyteller can take control over those past events because they are the ones who get to define the meaning of those events for an audience and for themselves. This is all to say that if something in your past is troubling you, telling that story out loud can be very helpful.

Sarah worked with me on a few different kinds of stories over a couple of semesters before she revealed to me that she had been struggling with an eating disorder for almost a decade. "I'm anorexic *and* bulimic. What can I say? I'm an overachiever," Sarah joked as we talked. Dark humor aside, she felt she was finally getting a handle on the problem, and she was ready to tell the story in public. She thought it would do herself and possibly others some good to hear her story. The performance laid out a series of disturbing episodes that described how her condition began, how it manifested itself, and her road to recovery. Sarah had been deceiving the people around her about her disorder and deceiving herself about the seriousness of her problem. Composing a story about these experiences was a revelatory process for her, bringing these deceptions into the light. All her past behavior seemed to have an intractable grip on her present. For Sarah, her eating disorder was very much out of her control, but telling her story gave her a sense of power over the story, so that it had less power over her. However, it is important to note that Sarah waited until she felt secure enough to tell the story. She did not try to put her experience on stage while she was still entrenched in self-deception.

Storytelling can also help us make sense of the present. Many stories we tell about ourselves are charged with meaning, such that they either explicitly or implicitly offer a sort of program for living. Thinking through experiences and articulating them in a story can help the speaker understand how they should behave in the here and now. Theatre and storytelling have the wonderful quality of being a site where we can rehearse possibilities, where we can try out our actions before we put them into play in the so-called "real world."

I worked on a story like this with Gal, who had moved from Israel to the US with his family years ago. Gal talked about a series of encounters with a professor who engaged in a disturbing pattern of cultural essentialism, assuming everything Gal did reflected his Jewish and Israeli heritage. Gal's story skewered the professor's behavior and, in doing so, illuminated how bad cultural essentialism can make people feel. He had not confronted his professor in the midst of these episodes. It was only after the fact, in the context of the story, that he was able to publicly critique his professor's actions. He wasn't able to question his professor at the time, but composing the story left Gal with a model for speaking up against this kind of cultural essentialism when he encounters it now. The story also deconstructed cultural essentialism for the audience, encouraging them to interrogate their own behavior in the moment. In the end, the story helped Gal sort through a topic relevant to him in real time.

Telling stories about yourself can also help you imagine the future and redefine how you characterize yourself. For better or worse, the stories we tell about ourselves help to define our sense of who we are and where we are going. Thus, taking control of that narrative can help us take control of the direction of our future. As Linda Park-Fuller argues, "Because that process is ongoing, inventive, and unique process not only reveals the truth; it creates it" (27). This creation of a new truth can be understood as the evocation, or bringing forth, of an as yet absent future (Park-Fuller 29).

Anna came to me, wanting to tell a story about her struggle with and gradual acceptance of dyslexia. As a child, Anna was very bright, but she struggled with reading and was placed in remedial courses. The narrative of her trajectory was set for her: she wasn't meant to amount to much in life. However, Anna found ways to manage her dyslexia. She became a successful student and a prolific writer and storyteller. At the end of her story about dyslexia, Anna imagines her future aloud: a published author, walking through city streets, on the way to see a production of a play she's written. She invites the audience to imagine the scene along with her. In this story, the possibility of Anna's eventual success becomes the catharsis that resolves the struggles in her past. At the time of this writing, Anna is investigating graduate school programs to keep pursuing her goal of writing professionally.

Sarah, Gal, and Anna all told stories about feelings that they had, more or less, been keeping to themselves. In each case, telling their stories aloud to an audience left them feeling better about those experiences and about themselves. This leads us to a final personal motive for telling stories on stage: it feels good. In many artistic contexts, cultural norms tend to emphasize a slavish devotion to performing for others for their sake or a myopic investment in craft above all else. We valorize people who "suffer for their art," as if suffering is a prerequisite for making good work. However, I believe the truth is that most artists—and perhaps performers in particular—take great personal pleasure in their work. Elizabeth Bell sponsors a similar position, arguing for an orientation to performance that de-centers the text and re-centers the "material pleasures of performance as a tensely negotiated economy of exchange among performer, audience, and text" (100). In other words, the pleasure of the dynamic interchange between all the participants is a value and an end in and of itself. I began this Chapter with Daniel and his story about breaking into his high school, getting caught, and not learning any sort of lesson. As we talked the story over, we agreed that even though his story didn't have a neat moral, it was about something important. The story was a vivid snapshot that captured one of those moments in your life when you are young and free (and maybe a little reckless) before more adult responsibilities set in. Daniel relished the opportunity to tell a very funny story and to paint a picture of that moment in time. Slowly, as we worked on his story, I realized that Daniel's didn't need a moral. His story was a slice of life, a love letter to being young and foolish. Making the audience laugh and giving them a glimpse at the jubilant recklessness of youth gave Daniel (and the audience) a lot of pleasure, and that was enough. I learned that he did not need to learn anything, and there did not need to be a moral for his story to speak directly to the human condition.

At this point, I need to mention that some critics think telling personal stories on stage is a selfish endeavor. Some people argue that it is narcissistic for a performer to get on stage with any expectation that they get something out of the experience or that the audience be in any way obliged to witness a performance that is useful to the performer. For those who feel personal storytelling is selfish or self-indulgent, we might turn the tables on the critic. "Why do we presume," Craig Gingrich-Philbrook asks, "we are entitled to a world in which we are never troubled by a person getting a little better in public?" ("Therapy" 139). Is it also not selfish for an audience member to suppose that stages and performance spaces are only reserved for purposes that serve the audience first? The truth is that these two goals—serving the performer and serving the audience—are rarely mutually exclusive. What works for audiences—what they find moving—is often also what is most edifying for the performer. While these criticisms have little merit when applied to well-crafted performance, it is important to remember that this opinion is out there.

Ideological Motives

We also tell stories in service of ideological motives. When I say "ideology" I am using that word in a specific way, as it was used by French philosopher Louis Althusser. He used the word "ideology" to describe "the imaginary relationship of individuals with the real conditions of their existence" (36). These so-called "imaginary relationships" are imaginary in the sense that they are not tangible, but they are entirely real in the sense that they have a significant effect on people. Most of us have heard the old saying, "sticks and stones can break my bones, but words will never hurt me," and we also know that is nonsense. Or, perhaps more charitably, that old saying is a wish more than a statement of fact because words, which are also imaginary, hurt us all the time. Things that are not "real," in the strictest sense, can still exert a great deal of influence over us. Ideology describes a set of imaginary social relations that shape who we are as people and ensure our commitment to social order. For instance, the rules at school are made up by teachers and administrators, they don't exist in nature like a tree or a rock. But if you violate the rules, there can be real implications—like when Daniel and his friends were suspended for breaking into the school. One simple way of thinking about ideology is that these imaginary social relations state and reinforce messages about what is true, what is important, and how we should behave. These social relations are set up in institutions like churches, schools, clubs, and, importantly for us, media—including, I contend, the stories we create *and* consume.

All stories have an ideological dimension. Whether intentional or not, the stories we tell can either reinforce or challenge assumptions about what it means to be a person navigating the world. In many cases, such as animal fables or mythology, the message is a metaphorical representation of ideology. Think of the story of the ant and the grasshopper. The ant diligently prepares for winter while the grasshopper plays all day. When the snow flies, the grasshopper is in trouble while the ant is safe and sound. The message that "hard work is necessary to survive" comes through loud and clear. In the case of personal stories we tell about ourselves, the ideological content is usually more literal; social relations are at the center of the story. Think about Sarah, Gal, and Anna's stories earlier in this chapter. Each one offered an ideological point of view. But whether ideology is represented metaphorically or literally, ideology is present in all stories. With thoughtful attention to the story you are creating, you can sponsor an ideological message that fits with your own values. Thinking back to Daniel's story at the beginning of this chapter, ideology was my main concern with his story. I was worried that if Daniel told his story with no moral, no lesson at the end, his message would seem at best ambiguous and at worst it would seem he was encouraging the audience to engage in underage drinking and trespassing. And, while Daniel wasn't all that opposed to those things, that wasn't really the reason he was telling the story. Ultimately, we made sure to emphasize his friendships in the story, his insecurity in his ability to impress a person he found attractive, and his desire to rebel against authority—all hallmarks of being a young person. By shifting the focus of the story away from committing misdemeanors and toward the delicious feeling of youthful freedom, Daniel was able to ensure that he was highlighting a set of social relations that were important to him. Daniel could have told his story with the sole intent of getting a laugh but, by orienting himself to the ideological value of his story, he was able to make the audience laugh while making the story about the things that moved us in our youth.

Let's look at another, more personal, example of the implicit ideological content in the stories we tell. Laila was working on a story about her first kiss. A lot of people have good, cringe-worthy first kiss stories. They often capture something meaningful about what it's like to grow up, and they are stories most people can relate to. Laila hadn't kissed anyone well into her teenage years, and she'd begun to feel self-conscious, sensing social pressure, and her own desire around that topic. So, when she met an older guy who showed interest in her at a party, she wound up going on a date with him. After some confusion and a bad movie, they were parked in his truck. She'd been waiting for this moment for a long time, and when he went in for the kiss, it wound up sloppy, slobbery, and a little bit aggressive. She didn't feel harmed or unsafe, but she was deeply disappointed that her first kiss was such a bad one. By performing her anxious desire to be kissed, Laila subtly revealed something to the audience about the cultural conditions that made it feel so urgent. Culture uses romantic or sexual experience as a kind of benchmark that indicates growth. Conversely, if you've never been kissed, you don't feel you're meeting those benchmarks. You can be left feeling like you're lacking if your experience doesn't meet the imaginary expectations that culture offers us. Laila was willing to go on a date that didn't really seem like a good idea just to appease that social pressure. The bad kiss ends up as a metaphor for the ways things can turn out when we give in to unnecessary expectations. Laila's story points at gender politics inherent in cultural systems without being heavy-handed.

On the other hand, sometimes you may want to be very explicit about an ideological point of view. One important function of ideology in storytelling is the possibility of ideological intervention into the dominant, overarching stories that culture tells about us and about others. Another French philosopher, Jean-François Lyotard, calls these stories the "master narrative," or the big story we tell (and are told) about culture. This master narrative can be particularly troubling for people who don't fit within it, as the master narrative works to keep them on the margins. Personal narrative performances can push back against the master narrative, bringing those marginalized voices to the center of the conversation. Fred Corey argues that "the personal narrative is one way of disturbing the master narrative, and through the performative dimensions of the personal narrative, the individual is able to disrupt—and, dare I say *rewrite*—the master narrative" (250). In this way, personal stories can be an ideological intervention.

Sasha's story offers a good example of an ideological intervention through narrative. Sasha had gone through an "abstinence only" sex education program in high school and she did not enjoy it—to say the least. The program taught that the only safe sex was no sex and that engaging in premarital sex made women, for lack of a better word, unclean. As a young person, Sasha was used to listening to authority figures and doing what she was told, but this all felt wrong to her. From her point of view, the "abstinence only" program was sending all the wrong messages to young people. The story she told about this experience was designed to show just how ridiculous and harmful the program was. Eventually, Sasha, her mother, and a group of concerned citizens petitioned the school board to replace the program. When she told the story in public, she even handed out copies of a link to a petition the audience could sign. Sasha's story was driven by her desire to intervene into this program and promote a more sex-positive worldview.

As you can see from Sasha's story, personal storytelling is an excellent way to put more of what you want into the world. It can provide vivid, heart-rending, relatable evidence of experience that can be persuasive in ways that statistics or data never could. This is good for storytellers who want to use their stories to shape the understanding of their audience. However, the fact that all stories carry ideological content means that all storytellers are responsible for the content of the stories that they tell. It is important that you be reflective about the values you are sponsoring in your story.

I worked with a student in a class who told a story about getting hurt on a cruise ship and winding up in a tiny medical facility with a large nurse. This student tried to draw the maximum amount of laughter out of the juxtaposition of the large nurse and the small space. In the end, it felt like he was making fun of the nurse's size. It wasn't a particularly thoughtful or charitable attitude to adopt toward the story, even though it might have gotten some cheap laughs. This student was reinforcing and reproducing problematic sizeist cultural relations about women and bodies. I don't think that's what the student meant to do, but sufficient attention had not been paid to the ideological dimension of the story.

Academic and Professional Motives

The academic discipline of performance studies has become ground zero for the use of personal narratives as academic discourse. This trend has been part of the "performance turn" away from empirical evidence and toward the subjective lived experience of individuals as evidence of cultural and communicative phenomena. Personal storytelling is appealing in the context of performance studies for several reasons. First, as I often tell my students, many so-called objective empirical methods offer insights that are a mile wide, but only an inch deep. Conversely, individual narratives lack the generalizability of larger data sets but offer a deeper, richer, and first-hand account of the topic at hand. This deep evidence of experience can be far more revealing than a large set of data that lacks rich detail. Furthermore, personal stories require the teller to be held accountable for their own biases and point of view, in a way that other, more objective methods of expressing scholarship do not. In fact, the tendency for so-called objective scholarship to ignore its own blind spots is one major gap that narrative-driven methods seek to fill. Imagine, for example, telling a moving story about dealing with a cancer diagnosis. The texture, detail, and emotion of that story could capture the reality of the illness in a way that empirical data may not.

Another practical reason for infusing scholarship with personal stories, is that it can enliven what might otherwise be a dry and less appealing presentation. Several years ago, I led a group of students in teaching a series of workshops on storytelling to girls at The Global Village Project, a school for refugee girls. The task was daunting: the girls had various levels of English proficiency and they came from a variety of cultural backgrounds. My students and I devised a curriculum to help the girls understand story structure and, importantly, feel more comfortable standing on their feet and speaking in front of a group. We've all heard that old cliché, "my students teach me just as much as I teach them," but in this case I'm certain it was true. In facilitating the curriculum, my students learned a great deal about teaching, storytelling, and cultural sensitivity. Together, we applied for support to travel to an international conference on service learning and community engagement. The students crafted a performance that interwove their own stories of teaching at The Global Village Project. The result was a conference presentation that vividly depicted not just what happened, but how it felt to work with the girls. Their performance helped to transport the audience to the school and make the experience real for them. The assembled audience offered positive comments about the content and the charming and evocative method of delivery. It was much more effective than simply giving a dry academic presentation on the subject.

Beyond the insulated world of the academy, personal storytelling has value in a variety of professional contexts. It is common these days to see a tab labeled "Our Story" at the top of most business' webpage. From shoe companies to realtors, businesses have learned the importance of connecting the product to a narrative that makes the product special. Thinking back to our conversation about ideology in storytelling earlier in this chapter, connecting a product to a story also means connecting your product to an ideology. One can easily imagine a line of healthy snacks designed for kids by a mother who struggled to find healthy food for her kids. This kind of story helps the product transcend mere commerce and express a set of ideological values the purchasing public can resonate with. This is not only true for products; individuals also often connect their public professional persona with a particular narrative. For instance, during his first campaign for President, Barack Obama told his personal story time and again: the son of a single mother, a child of two cultures, a success story no one expected. The story helped voters understand who he was and, perhaps, why he was different from many politicians they'd encountered before. Furthermore, personal testimonials—a kind of narrative in their own right—have long been used to demonstrate the efficacy of a given product. Whether it is whiter teeth, cleaner shirts, or a safer home, businesses use the stories of satisfied customers to drive home the value of their product. Understanding how these testimonials work and helping people to craft them can, in turn, help to increase sales. Recently, I reconnected with a former student who told me a story about applying for a job as a paralegal assisting with immigration cases. At her interview, the skeptical employer asked, "how did your bachelor's degree in theatre and performance studies prepare you for this position?" She went on to explain that she had learned excellent writing, speaking, organizational, and research skills but, most importantly, she said, "all immigration cases are about telling a story and I know exactly how to do that." Needless to say, she got the job. You can probably think of your own examples of places where personal stories emerge in professional contexts. The point is: understanding and crafting personal stories has applications far beyond the classroom or the stage.

In this chapter, we've spent some time thinking about why we tell personal stories. To be honest, there is a long list of reasons people put their stories on stage. What we've discussed here hits some of the most important points on that list. When you can find ways to tell a story that you enjoy telling, that an audience enjoys hearing, and that puts more of what you believe into the world, you've found your own reasons.

Questions to Consider

1 What ideological positions are most important to you? Make a list of as many of those positions as you can.
2 What stories have you found persuasive? What stories have taught you something you did not know before? What stories changed the way you look at a subject? Make a list of those stories that have moved you.
3 Read Sasha's story about abstinence-only sex education. What strategies does she use to help you understand her point of view?

"Sex Ed"
Created and Performed by Sasha Ashley

We shuffled into the big, dark theater one by one, giggling and laughing because we were about to learn about what I had been waiting for since I first saw Legolas in The Lord of the Rings. *[Pauses gaze fixed]* S-E-X. Sex. "Ooh, we can't wait to learn about sex," we all said in unison.

We were in the middle of summer health and PE, which was this awesome program where you got to take the boring classes like health and PE before ninth grade to make room for the more exciting classes like jewelry making, or AP lit, AP calculus, AP trig.

But we had just come back from learning about how you take cough syrup. Pretend I have a shoelace. *[Takes imaginary shoelace]* Okay? So you tie it to your shoelace, and then you spin it around, *[Spins around shoelace]* and all of the hallucinogens go to the top. So while half of us were excited about sex, the other half were excited about legal drug use. Basically, everyone was really excited.

Suddenly, a spotlight licked the stage and there stood a big, bold, aggressively old white woman in her thirties, at least, raising up her hand

[Raises hand] to show us her 'I Won't Until I Do' bracelet, as a gym teacher walked down the aisles to hand each of us our very own blue rubber bracelets. I won't, as in have sex, and I do, as in marriage.

We were there to learn about abstinence-based sex education. If you don't know what abstinence-based sex education is, I'm glad, because it's stupid. She scanned the crowd, checking for our bracelets. As she towered over her audience of 14-year-olds, she was ready. I, on the other hand, was not ready for what I was about to experience.

I have this thing where, when I am around authority figures that I don't really know, I get really, really quiet. So as I, very quietly, sat in my seat waiting to learn about sex, very loudly, stood on the stage ready to teach us. She started with the most important part, *[Spreads legs bends down]* "If you have sex, you will get pregnant, and your baby will *[motions birthing]* ruin your life and end your life. You will regret it, even when you are a grandparent."

I was like, "I don't know about that, because life's never ruined. That's what my mom said." But before I could finish that thought I heard, *[Squats down again lowers voice]* "Birth control. If you think you're going to use the pill, you're going to get pregnant anyway, and you might as well put a big red A right here because you are a slut. Using a condom during sex is as dangerous as hanging off the edge of a cliff with a frayed rope. It breaks."

I was like, "I really don't know about that because my mom said 98 efficacy rate, and I just think…" But before I finish that thought, the projector lit up behind her to begin a 20-minute slideshow presentation consisting of incredibly graphic images—many of you might remember this—of untreated STDs, as she suggested that this is what all STDs look like and, "If you get one, you will definitely die."

[Squats down again]

"If you have sex, you are having sex with everyone that person has had sex with. Do you hear me? Everyone those people have had sex with. If any of them have an STD, and you know they do, congratulations, you do too now."

Oh, my God, she was so right. I was not a girl, but I was not yet a woman, and I was not ready to die.

The images burned into my mind we like you know eggplant and peach emojis? Okay, well the peaches were bruised and moldy, and the eggplants were deformed, I think, and purple. But before I had to finish that thought, I heard, *[resumes squat]* "Okay, kids. Everyone come to the stage." So as we walked up to the stage, she handed us each one single Hershey's kiss, and then said, "Okay, okay, okay. Now take the kiss and put it in your mouth. Okay? Now suck on it, but don't chew." Which, honestly, was the best piece of sex education I got that whole summer.

She then told us to take out the brown, mushy, wet chocolate and wrap it up in our tin foil again, and then trade it with the person next to us. She then said, "Do you want to put it in your mouth now?" We said, "No, we don't want to put it in our mouth now." "Exactly. If you think putting a piece of candy in your mouth after someone is gross, imagine someone's vagina." So, I did.

But before I could finish that thought, we were all shuffled to the back of the stage while my friend Sarah was brought to the front and given a big, thick, clear piece of tape, and told to put it onto the arms of four different boys. Then, as she stood there at the front of the stage holding her dirty, tainted, no longer valuable, piece of tape, the speaker said to the girls, and only the girls, that, "This is what happens to you when you have sex. The more people you have sex with, the dirtier you become, and all you can do with used tape is throw it away."

Even at 14, all I could think was, "What if you're raped? What if you're just ready to have sex and you're old enough to make your own decisions without feeling ashamed of your body? What if you just want to have autonomy over your own body? Why can't I have sex with Legolas if I want to?" After school that day, as I sat in my mother's red minivan, I engaged in some quiet reflections.

I thought about how uncomfortable it made me when she compared us to chewing gum that could only be chewed once. I remembered how angry it made me when she compared us to white picket fences and said that, "Every time you had sex, another nail was hammered into us. While you could take out the nail, you could never fill the hole." I remembered how upset it made me when she compared us to flowers, but told us that, "When we have sex, all of our petals are plucked out and no one wants a flower with no petals."

I peered across the seat in front of me to see my mother's face. "Mom, I think that some moral boundaries are being crossed at school, and I'm not quite old enough to really effectively fight back, and it's like they got me at the perfect age that I'm just impressionable enough that I might believe them." My mother stopped the car, *[motions stopping a car]* "Daughter, tell me everything."

So, I did. I talked to my mom, and my mom talked to me, and I talked to my mom, and my mom talked to me. Suddenly, it is June of 2017 and we are formally addressing the school board about the effects of abstinence-based sex education on survivors of rape and sexual assault. If you guys open your programs, you'll see, or if you already have, there's a pink slip of paper in there with a website, an address.

This address is for a petition that my mother and I have started. Well, we started it, but we're working with a lot of other awesome people to fight abstinence-based sex education in Gwinnett County. So if this is something that matters to you, then we could really, really use your help. If you want to find out more, I urge you to stay for the talkback after the show.

Here's the future I'd like to see. Imagine a world where students are taught by teachers who care about their students and want them to do well. A world where students are taught consent, and that LGBTQ kids both exist and have different needs than their straight friends. A world where facts and statistics reign. Most importantly, a world where if I'm compared to a flower, it's not because my petals have been plucked and I'm to be thrown away, but because I'm beautiful.

3 "The Goat Is on the Roof": Choosing What to Talk About

When Courtney was a kid, her mom would take her on a women's spiritual retreat every summer at a farm in North Carolina. As the only kid at the farm, Courtney's only playmate was her golden retriever, Goliath. At the end of one particular day, after Courtney and Goliath had a big batch of adventures on the farm, they sat on the porch of the farmhouse with her mom. They watched as the goats in the yard jumped on the roof of a little shed and hopped off, as goats do. Courtney's mom broke the silence, saying, "the goat is on the roof." It was one of those odd turns of phrase that takes on significance in a family. Over the years, when things got tough, one of them would say, "the goat is on the roof" and they'd be reminded that hope was on the horizon and things were going to be all right. After all, "all is right in a goat's world when she is on the roof." Years passed, and as happens, Goliath got sick and eventually he had to be let go. The last time they took Goliath to the vet's office, Courtney's mom was a wreck, weeping over the loss of their dog. In her grief, she lashed out at Courtney, who was stoic and silent. Why, her mother asked, was she not more broken up over this tragic event? Courtney replied that she knew Goliath was in a better place now, able to run and play in ways that illness had denied him. "The goat," Courtney told her mother, "is on the roof."

Courtney told me this story, pretty much this way, when we first sat down to work on her performance. The loss of her dog, Goliath, was a moment that loomed large in her childhood. But, hanging over that story, was the fact that her relationship with her mother was often fraught with difficulty. Originally, Courtney had only intended to make the story about her beloved dog. Along the way, we realized that the story was truly about her relationship with her mother and that we could enter that part of the story through the story about her dog, visiting the farm, and the goat on the roof. Courtney had begun with a simple idea and discovered a story with deeper implications along the way. Her journey with this story illustrates the fact that you need not know what a story is truly about when you begin working on it. To get started, you need only know that something about the subject speaks to you.

Sometimes, stories from our lives just unfold in front of us and it seems obvious what we should say about them. Some events, like a birthday party

DOI: 10.4324/9781003039266-3

for example, have a clearly delineated beginning, middle, and end, making the structure of the story clear. Some people have a big thing in their lives that is begging to come out—like Sarah's struggle with eating disorders in the last chapter. At other times, it is not so obvious what we should talk about. Ask enough people what they want to talk about on stage, and you'll hear many, many people say, "there is nothing interesting about me. I don't have any stories to tell." That is simply not true. Everyone is interesting.

Once I was talking to a group of high school students on this subject, and I told them that there is something interesting about everyone. I told them I would prove it. I picked a young woman at random out of the audience. "You," I said to her, "what did you do last night?" She replied, "Nothing, I just got pizza with my family." "And who drove you to get the pizza?" I asked her. "My dad drove us," she said. "Now," I said to her, "I need to ask you an important question: is your dad cool?" Everyone chuckled at the question. "No, no he's not," she laughed. Why not? "Well, he drives this old beat-up van and he always wears hockey jerseys …" and she went on. Obviously, in just a few seconds, we were already on to something interesting. That's because everyone is interesting.

When people tell you that they have nothing to talk about, what they really mean is that they can't *see* how interesting their lives are, and they don't *think* their stories are worth telling. Perhaps it is an exercise in the social convention of humility that suggests we should not assume anything about ourselves is important. Maybe it is a fear of self-disclosure. Whatever might be keeping you from thinking you don't have anything interesting to say, I assure you: you have stories, and your stories are worth telling.

All stories, especially personal stories, are about the same thing. All stories are about what it means to be a person in the world. You are the only person who can determine what you want to say. In order to figure out what you want to say, we begin by thinking through strategies for identifying meaningful moments in your life that might make good stories. Next, we'll look at how you, like Courtney, can uncover the metaphorical content of your story. Finally, we'll look at particularly difficult topics and how you can approach them.

Stories Derived from Social Drama

One way of identifying a good subject for a story is to look for moments of drama in your life. Anthropologist Victor Turner was a central figure in helping the academic world view human behavior as performance. Among his many insights, was the model of social drama, which offers a framework for understanding what happens when something goes wrong in social relations. We can lay Turner's model of social drama over everyday problems to better understand those problems through the lens of drama. Turner's model of social drama offers us a way to map our own experiences and understand how they may be extracted from the continuity of our memories and become something we can talk about on stage.

Turner's model has four stages: breach, crisis, redressive action, and reintegration. The first stage, breach, is of particular interest to us. A breach is a moment of disruption between a particular person or group and the larger social order. When we depart from the normal, rule-governed expectations of our culture or community, a breach often ensues. The departure may be as simple as acting weird in middle school or as dramatic as getting into a bar fight. In either case, social norms are disrupted. In the second stage, crisis, the breach widens, and things generally get worse. People respond to the breach, and those responses are usually not positive. If, for example, you breached social norms by acting weird in middle school, you might have been teased by your peers—a widening of the breach. In stage three, redressive action, those involved in the events seek to remedy the situation. The person responsible for the breach might apologize or the social order might act, sanctioning the disruptive actor. For example, the bar fight combatants might come to their senses and try to deescalate the situation, or the bartender might step in to break up the fight. In the final stage, reintegration, the breach and the person (or persons) who caused it are reintegrated into the social order or pushed further outside the social order. Sometimes, the social order makes accommodations to accept what was once considered a breach. Whatever the case, this final stage seeks to bring things back into harmony. Imagine, for example, the two people in our fictional bar fight making up and sharing a beer together. Let's look at an example of social drama as it plays out in a specific story.

In his story, Matt went camping with his girlfriend and their pals. Along the way, he somehow lost a knife that belonged to his girlfriend's recently deceased father. Losing the knife creates a moment of breach: Matt has done something he was not supposed to do. The gap widens as his girlfriend fumes at him, he feels guilty, and the whole band of campers derail their trip. They return to the mountain so Matt can search for the knife. Energized by the embarrassment at what he's done and the fear of being alone in the woods, Matt attempts redressive measures by frantically racing to search the woods for the missing knife. Finally, Matt finds the knife, and his girlfriend forgives him for his mistake. The breach is repaired, and Matt and his girlfriend are reintegrated into a happy couple.

As you can see, this moment of breach provided Matt with a good story to tell and an opportunity to reflect on himself and his own behavior. The story also acts as its own kind of redressive measure, rewriting the event into a funny, sweet story rather than a moment of thoughtlessness. The audience is also implicitly invited to reflect on their own past mistakes and how they might be rewritten in their memory. Most of the time, stories about something going wrong provide a natural narrative arch because they follow the model that Turner identified. Good stories are often embedded in the moments when we try, and fail and must find a way to move on.

Stories Derived from Noetic Moments

In Latin, the word *noesis* refers to "understanding" or "intellect." In other words, it refers to things that seem to reside, primarily, in our minds. A performance artist friend of mine, Violet Juno, uses the phrase "noetic moments" as a kind of shorthand to refer to moments where something radically comes to our consciousness, or something suddenly becomes visible to us as knowledge. These moments do not always feel as if they are part of a surrounding story, perhaps because the moment shines so brightly, so to speak, that you can't see precisely what led to it. At other times, it is very clear what led to these moments of realization. Searching your past for noetic moments can be another way to arrive at a good topic for your story. The network of events leading to and then following noetic moments very often make for good stories.

Sarah came to me with one such moment: the moment she and a friend accidentally burned down a large portion of woods behind her family's home. The moment, of course, held a significant place in Sarah's childhood memory, but was the moment really part of a larger story? The woods burning down was an event, but not a story per se. I asked her how it was that the two girls came to burn down the woods. Sarah explained that they were around the age of 12 and had set out to pretend to go camping in the woods behind the house. Sarah was, according to her own description, a country kid who was used to running around in the woods while her friend lived in town and saw country life as a novelty. As it turned out, Sarah's friend was also a very popular girl and, as we all know, feeling like you fit in with the popular kids is a powerful motivator when you're young. As they pretended to camp, Sarah started a fire to impress her friend. Not long after, Sarah's brother entered the picture and tried to make the fire bigger by throwing cardboard on the blaze, scattering the flames, and igniting the trees in the process. Eventually, the fire department put out the fire and everyone was fine. But it remained a vivid memory in Sarah's mind. Seeing how much her friend enjoyed the woods and then nearly losing them brought Sarah's love for her country home to her consciousness in a way she had previously not considered. The story also dramatized Sarah's desire to be liked by her popular friend—a feeling many people can relate to. The fire in the woods was, in and of itself, a moment, but the events before and after the fire and the motives that caused it gave the story shape.

It is worth noting that you may be able to map Turner's model of social drama over a story like Sarah's that was inspired by a noetic moment. These categories are not discrete from one another but, rather, different ways of discovering ideas. I should also mention that noetic moments need not be moments of crisis per se. Instead, they may be experiences that spring to the forefront of your mind, and ask us to speak about them.

Kristi and I worked for weeks on a lovely story about her running away from home (well, just down the driveway) when she was a very young child.

The story was all ready to go before our spring showcase performance when her beloved grandfather passed away. Kristi was heartbroken and filled with memories of her grandfather, so much so that it dominated her thinking. A few days before the show, she came to me and said, "I need to talk about my grandfather." As we'll discuss later in this chapter, telling stories about emotional episodes you're right in the middle of is a big risk and usually not advisable. Kristi was willing to take the risk; we sketched out the rough outline of the story, and a few days later she performed it in our showcase. While her grandfather's death was sad, it was not a crisis per se and not something that could be rectified with redressive measures. But it was a moment where something was made visible, namely her grandfather's irrepressible character and love for his family. Kristi captured her grandfather's playful, exuberant spirit and brought plenty of people in the audience to tears. Most importantly, she was allowed to say a big, public, performative goodbye to someone she loved. In Kristi's case, the moment on her mind—the death of her grandfather—was so pressing that it became her only and best choice at that time.

Stories Driven by Issues

Yet another way to approach the question, "what *should* I talk about?" is to ask yourself, "what do I *want* to talk about?" Answers to this question come in many forms. There may be a pressing social issue that hits close to home for you, such as homophobia, racism, or sexual violence. Or there may be something about you as an individual that makes you unique—a central part of your identity that you want to bring before an audience. For the most part, these stories driven by issues work in the opposite direction from the stories we've discussed thus far. In most cases, a story reveals itself, and the story-teller works to identify the larger and meaningful themes of the story. In the case of stories driven by issues, the teller begins with a theme and works backward to construct a story that illustrates the theme. Sometimes, the process is a combination of both approaches. Obviously, determining what story to tell by identifying the issue that drives it is directly tied to the discussion of ideology in Chapter 2.

We first met Gal in Chapter 2. In addition to being an immigrant from Israel, Gal is also a surprisingly big, tall person. He's not just tall; he has big hands, big legs, and big shoulders. He can fill an average doorway with his impressive size. It is the first thing people notice about him, but it is not always easy being different. Gal also loved professional wrestling. He liked the stories, the characters, and found it to be a fun distraction from everyday life. When Gal went about figuring out the first story, he was drawn to talk about how his large size has often made him feel like an outsider. He literally did not fit in with other people. He intertwined his own experiences with those of one of his heroes, professional wrestler Andre the Giant. Gal's story paralleled his life with Andre's and allowed him to talk about a personal issue that was important to him. In this case, Gal drew on a number of episodes from his life that typified his experience as a big person, rather than focusing on a single coherent narrative. This approach put this issue of feeling like an outsider in the foreground, and the narratives functioned to support the case he made.

Determining What Your Story Is About

When I ask new storytellers, "What is your story about?" they will almost without fail tell me about the events as they unfold in the story. I try to listen patiently, but sometimes I stop them and say, "You're telling me what happens in the story. I want to know what it is *about*." Uncovering the potential hidden meaning inside the stories we tell is, for me, the most interesting part of developing a new story. Determining what a story is about is the part of this process that most feels like therapy and the part that is most revealing. The distinction between what happens in a story and what a story is about is the difference between plot and theme.

The plot of a story refers to the actions that unfold inside the story. When we say someone is "plotting a heist" we mean that they are arranging the steps necessary for that crime to take place. A story's structure is the arrangement of the events that make up the plot into an order that the teller (and hopefully the audience) find effective in communicating the story. Any series of events can be interpreted in a variety of ways. In fact, it is fair to say that a series of events has no meaning until the storyteller, situated within their own cultural context, interprets the meaning of those events for themselves. The storyteller may choose to relay some events in the plot and leave out others to accentuate a particular interpretation of events. The interpretation of events, giving meaning to the things that happen in stories, offers up the theme of a particular story.

The theme of a story is how I describe the overarching meaning of the story. That does not mean, of course, that a story can or should be only about one thing. Stories should, for the most part, have a theme that the audience can identify. One way we can imagine the theme of a story is by thinking of it as the thesis of a story. When writing an essay, all the things that you write ought to support the overarching thesis you set out at the beginning. Similarly, storytellers select and arrange elements of the plot to accentuate a particular point they are trying to make. Conceiving of your story as having a thesis is very much like the moral of a folktale or a fairytale that you may have learned as a child. In this case, the thesis-as-moral is usually structured as an assertion or a statement of policy. In other words, it is a statement about something the storyteller thinks others should or should not do. The story, in turn, illustrates this assertion. One can imagine any number of common assertions like this: don't try to be someone you're not, treasure what you have because you can lose it, and respect other people. We can easily imagine stories that would illustrate these statements. This sort of thesis is often explicitly stated. However, you may discern your thesis but never explicitly state it in the story, choosing instead to let it guide your choices without saying it out loud. This is often the best choice because it encourages the audience to actively participate in the meaning-making.

The theme of a particular story need not be a thesis or other affirmative statement. Often, the theme of a story is much more abstract and offers no assertion of policy or action. Rather, the theme may be a kind of meditation on a particular subject. Remember, for instance, Daniel's story about breaking into his high school? That story had no moral but, rather, offered a loving look at more-or-less harmless teenage rebellion. Self-discovery, anger, joy, grief, and the appreciation of beauty are just a few examples of themes in a story that are not, explicitly, driven by a particular thesis.

I had a student who told a heart-wrenching story about his family losing custody of his foster brothers and the ways the two boys had cracked open his sometimes-cynical heart. He brought the first version of this story to class on a Friday morning, right after the events of the story took place. He didn't warn us that he was about to share something so raw and personal, and the assembled students and I were floored by the tragedy and emotional honesty of the story. As we worked on the story together, we went through a few different ideas about how to end it. In one version, he created an explicit statement about what he learned from these events toward the end of the story. That version encouraged the audience to never take the people you love for granted and to let your heart love, even though it might get broken. This ending reflected the theme of the story but it felt too heavy-handed and a bit cliché. After much discussion, we decided to end the story with him simply leaving his brothers on that painful afternoon. We decided that not spelling out the message would make room for the audience to draw their own conclusions. The emotional journey of this story is so vivid that the theme of loss speaks for itself, it doesn't require any explanation.

In my view, allowing the theme of a story to remain abstract for the audience is often (though not always) desirable because it leaves space for the listeners to draw their own conclusions about the meaning of the story. Years ago, I placed a moratorium on the use of the phrase "I realized" in my student's stories. I did this for two reasons. First, it felt like each of them inserted this phrase in their story somewhere toward the end, right before revealing the theme, thesis, or moral of the story. If you saw a group of them perform together, the formula became clear and repetitive. Second, and more important than my fear of seeming repetitive, using that phrase meant the storyteller was about to concretely layout the specific meaning of the story for the audience. That left less room for the audience to draw their own conclusions, which meant they might end up feeling less involved in the process. In the most sophisticated expression of this process, storytellers carefully lay out remarks and events so that, by the end of the story, the audience draws precisely the conclusion the storyteller wants without having to be told to do so. I describe this process as the storyteller leading the audience on a journey and allowing the audience to take the final steps in the journey alone. When the audience does that final cognitive work for themselves, they feel deeply involved in the process.

Recognizing the Metaphorical Content of Stories

A metaphor is a rhetorical strategy that allows one thing, usually something familiar, to represent another thing, usually something less well-known. You may be most familiar with metaphor as a figure of speech often used in poetry, a medium famous for comparing things to other things. In Chapter 6, we'll discuss metaphors and their use as figures of speech in stories. Metaphors abound across artistic mediums, allowing images, events, characters, and so on to stand in for more abstract ideas. Storytellers describe and characterize events so that the audience comes to see those events as representative of some other symbolic meaning. In Courtney's story, the goat on the roof became a metaphor that meant things were going to be alright. The feeling that things will be alright is an abstract concept that we can't see, smell, hear, or touch. We can't pick it up and carry it with us, but if we concretize it with a clear defining image, like a goat on a roof, we can hold the feeling a little tighter. For the most part, art attempts to point at ineffable concepts— concepts that we can barely speak about without using metaphor. I suspect that if you could jump in a time machine and travel 100 years into the future, you would find that people would still be writing popular songs about what it feels like to fall in love. Falling in love is a feeling that is so universal, so powerful, and yet so abstract that human beings will never stop trying to put it into words, even though any attempt to put it into words will never fully capture it. But, nonetheless, we try. Like those love songs, people use stories to put feelings into words so that they can be shared among people. If you have identified a topic for a story, that does not mean that you have discovered the deeper metaphorical content of the story. That takes self-reflexivity and attention to the content of the story.

In order to identify the metaphorical content of a story you want to tell, you must first engage in honest self-reflexivity. Honest self-reflexivity is an attempt to step outside of yourself and see yourself—and the events around you—as others might see them. It also means that one not only looks back at their past, but does so with a critical, questioning eye that does not take that past for granted. Storytellers need to be able to see themselves as their audience sees them so they can adjust their performance to either fit with or diverge from those expectations. But, storytellers must also see themselves honestly so that they can determine what was going on in their past.

Corrine was still, on some lingering level, disappointed with her cousin. She was telling me about the time she'd been a flower girl in a family wedding at probably five years of age. Her cousin, who was two years old, was the second flower girl. They both had the same job: process ahead of the bride, spreading flowers along the aisle. Corrine took the job very seriously. In her mind, the role of the flower girls was at the center of the whole affair. Mind you, she was telling me this years later, she was probably just under 20 years old by then. The two-year-old cousin, predictably, didn't do her job correctly. She picked up the flowers Corrine spread along the aisle, she ran around, and generally acted like a two-year-old. Five-year-old Corrine was mortified. Years later, she was still a little bitter that her cousin had botched the job. Corrine was (and is!) talented, funny, and charismatic, but I couldn't help but chuckle at her indignation. "Corrine," I told her, "your cousin didn't ruin the wedding, I'm sure people thought she was adorable. This story isn't about how your cousin ruined your chance to be a flower girl, it's about how you took the whole thing too seriously." At first, she argued with me, doubling down on her assertion that her cousin had blown it. Eventually, she agreed and created a very funny version of the story where she played her indignation for comic effect, ironically underscoring how ridiculous it was to be angry at a two-year-old for acting her age. Corrine had to step outside of herself to see the situation as others might see it and, in doing so, found an entry point into the story that made it more interesting.

Beyond engaging in self-reflexivity, storytellers need to comb through the details of their story to discover clues as to what meaning it might hold. Something that may not have seemed important at the time may take on dramatic significance upon further reflection. Ryann and I worked on her story, about her difficulty accepting her stepfather and her disappointment in her biological father, for a long while. She resisted describing her conflict with her stepfather, perhaps because she didn't want to delve into those painful stories. One day, while we were working together, I asked her what sorts of things she did to act out and defy him. "Small, petty things," she said. She would stay out one minute past curfew, disappear for hours, wander around a store, and generally disobey him by going just an inch past the line. That day Ryann told me, "Basically, I would manufacture a situation where he would have to be a disciplinarian just so I could remind him he wasn't my real dad." Her minor transgressions and massive arguments with her stepfather were a redirection of her anger at her biological father. She was not aware this dynamic was happening as a teenager but, upon further reflection, realized what was really going on behind the scenes. It was a revelatory moment in the creation of her story when Ryann realized what those fights were really about. This kind of revelation makes the metaphorical meaning of these events visible to the storyteller and, ultimately, their audience.

Telling Difficult Stories

Many first-time storytellers leap to the immediate, intuitive conclusion that the best stories must necessarily be about the worst subjects. With this assumption in mind, they seek out painful topics to mine for material. It's true that difficult moments in our lives usually make good subjects for stories, but they are, by no means, the only subjects for stories. Several of the anecdotes I've related thus far have focused on difficult subjects like death, loss, compulsions, and so forth. However, we've also addressed more everyday subjects like first kisses, romance gone wrong, and childhood accidents. Not all stories need to be about the worst parts of our lives. Those stories are usually precious to us and deserve to be treated with care.

It is important, especially for first-time storytellers, to carefully consider whether or not they are ready to talk about deeply personal topics on stage. You may feel that you've dealt with a particular topic sufficiently to turn it into a story. However, standing up in front of people and speaking can be a vulnerable situation under the best circumstances. People often find that they can easily say something to one person but get rattled when they have to say it to a dozen people. It is usually a good idea to begin with a subject with lower stakes to gain confidence in the process of composition, rehearsal, and performance. After all, you would not want to drive a race car as fast as it can go the very first time you get behind the wheel. You want to be sure of your skills before you do something very difficult. That being said, you are the only person who can really decide whether or not you are ready to discuss a particular topic.

One way to decide whether or not you are ready to take on a difficult subject is to see how comfortable you are treating the subject as material for a story rather than as a painful part of your past. Nathan and I worked closely on a story about his father succumbing to cancer. His father was a great guy, as illustrated in part by the fact that he bought himself and both his children each their own copies of every *Harry Potter* book. One day in my office, Nathan told me that when the final book came out, his father was too weak to read it, so they got him an audio copy instead. Without thinking, I blurted out, "oh, that's great!" I quickly tried to recover, apologizing, and telling Nathan that I only meant that moment would be moving in the story. Nathan chuckled at my awkwardness; he agreed, and he understood. He was ready to look at these events as material for a story, even though they were deeply personal to him.

It is also important that you work to take care of your audience when it comes to story selection. For the most part, you should not tell a story that leaves the audience wondering whether you are okay with having told it. Their concern for your wellbeing will likely supersede their ability to make sense of the story. If they are uncertain that you are okay, you are implicitly inviting them to take care of you rather than think about the story. Not only is it unfair to implicitly ask an unsuspecting audience to take care of your feelings, they can't actually offer that care, so they're just stuck with your feelings of pain and anxiety. As I mentioned earlier, storytelling can be therapeutic, but it's not therapy.

I said at the start of this book, storytelling is the art of getting an audience to see, think, and feel the same thing at the same time. If you do that effectively, it can be a very moving experience. However, storytellers have an ethical obligation to think about what they are asking their audience to see, think, and feel. The vivid depiction of violence on stage, for example, can dredge up memories of similar violence in the attending audience members. You may be ready to tell a story about violence or abuse, but audience members may not be ready to hear it. In most cases, there is a simple way to make the audience aware of such content before a performance and give them the option to opt out of audiencing the story.

Years ago, we hosted a solo performer at our institution who gave a very compelling solo performance of an autobiographical narrative. The performer told us ahead of time that the story included depictions of violence. As the coordinator for the event, I asked to see a copy of the script before the performance, but she was unwilling to share it for a variety of reasons. As I watched the show the first night, I saw her vividly and powerfully describe a sexual assault that she had survived. The story was well told but, each night I watched the show, I saw women around me gripping the arm rests of their seats and slowly breaking into tears. It was clear to me that they were not just moved by the story; they were reliving their own traumas. This was not what I wanted the audience to take away from this evening of storytelling. I did not want to play a role in igniting these feelings among the attendees. I was ashamed that I had not done more to prepare the audience for what they saw. I could have insisted the artist give me a clearer picture of the content, so I knew how to proceed. I could have posted signs alerting the audience to the powerful content on the doors to the theater or the box office. The experience taught me an important lesson about taking care of audience members.

Sometimes the decision to talk about a difficult topic is not so clear. You'll meet Ben again in Chapter 8, he told a story about a friend who'd committed suicide. As we worked on the story, we debated whether or not he should tell the story at all, for fear that someone who was also thinking of harming themselves would get the wrong idea. We worried that telling the story might trigger painful memories for people in the audience who'd lost a loved one that way. We wrestled to find a way to care for the audience. In the end, we put a note in the program for the performance that one of the stories in the show mentioned suicide and, when Ben reached that part of the story, he repeated the phone number for the national suicide help line twice. We discussed these measures with the rest of the students in the ensemble, and we agreed that we'd taken reasonable steps to protect the audience.

If you want to tell a story with content that is difficult for audience members to hear, there are ways to allude to topics like violence or abuse without stating it explicitly. You can, for instance, take the listener right up to the moment, leaving no doubt about what is about to happen, and then cut away from the action. This strategy may be more effective than vividly describing violence because it allows the audience to invest their own imagination into the story, while also allowing them the ability to dictate how much they need to imagine.

In this chapter, we've looked at some ways to identify good subjects for stories, the themes and metaphors in those stories, and how to deal with difficult stories. With any luck, you've already got a few story ideas churning around in your head. In the next chapter, we will begin discussing how you can structure these ideas into a story.

Questions to Consider

1 Read Matt's story at the end of this chapter and map Victor Turner's model of social drama through the story. What was revealed to you about the story through that process?
2 What issues are important to you? Make a list of issues you've encountered in your life that you're moved to talk about.
3 Create a list of story ideas and pick a few that stand out to you. What themes and metaphors emerge to you as you think about them?

"A Knife in the Dark"
Created and Performed by Matt Siano

In the woods, all alone in the middle of the night, everything, every stick breaking, every shadow is a bear.

We were driving up this meandering mountain road on the Tennessee line. It'd been over two years since Megan Jance and I went on our first date. We went running out on the trails around Kennesaw Mountain, and we'd fallen over exhausted on a bale of hay, and watched the full moon rise in the cosmic ocean. And her blue-gray eyes caught the starlight in them. I'm going to save the rest of that story for me.

So our two-year anniversary had just passed, and many of you may already know that her dad, Big George, had just passed as well. So that weekend, we resolved to spend it in nature. We'd always felt the most connected with each other and the most connected with ourselves. And so we rounded up the kind of people you can bring on a wilderness expedition with two hours' notice and headed up the Jacks River Falls. Now Megan and I are passionate outdoors people. I would say enthusiastic outdoors people, but I am not necessarily always the most *[Uses air quotes]* prepared outdoors person. It's a shocker, right?

One time we drove three hours to North Carolina, hiked 13 miles, straight up the side of the mountain, and got up to the top only to realize we didn't have any water! We had a ukulele.

But this weekend, I was prepared. I had four liters of water on my back. As much food as Megan Jance's mom could cram into my bag. And Big George's knife hung on my hip. And we pulled into the trail head and we started into the five miles towards the waterfall where we'd be making camp. And we saw the sun set over the mountains and set the sky on fire over the ancient Appalachians as we marched on past the no camping signs.

The time keeps on ticking. And as dusk was setting in, we were passing over this dry riverbed. And then I realized we screwed up this time because I'd forgotten my flashlights. And the only light that we had between the four of us was one tiny LED flashlight, blinking as if to tap out in Morse code, "please put batteries in me."

So I pulled up my back straps, grabbed the little light, and I ventured forth into the dark forest. And as I walked, I heard like a "gggrrrrr" sound and I was like, "Oh, it's nothing, I'm going to keep walking." "grrrrrr" sound. I was like, "Megan, do you hear that sound? I can't hear anything." She's like, "No, I don't hear anything. And then we heard something like a "ggggrrrrrrrr".

[Freezes with eyes big and whispers] "Where's the flashlight? It's a bear." *[Looking scared eyes wide.]* "Can somebody Google what you're supposed to do with it. Be very still they can't see you if you don't move." And then my friend reminded us that there are no recorded bear attacks on groups of three or more people. And that was good enough for us. It was dark by the time we could hear the waterfall, where we found a perfect place to pitch camp right under a no camping sign. In our defense, it was a picture of a tent with a red line through it. And we were using hammocks. We were fine, really. So we set up our fire, which was remarkably easy to do in a drought. We hung our bear bag admittedly poorly. And we spent the night singing songs around the campfire.

We woke up the next morning, scrambled around on rocks, splashed around in the waterfall, and had the exact kind of weekend we needed to have. But time keeps on ticking. And so soon it was time to hike the five miles out of the trail and drive the hour down the meandering mountain road, laughing about all the good times we've had that weekend. And we pulled into the nearest town and feasted ourselves on the glories of civilization—yummm—chimichangas. *[Rubs belly.]*

"Hey Megan, I gave you your dad's knife when we got off the trail, right?" And the stars in her eyes went supernova. And she said, "No, Matt, you did not give me my dad's knife." And we pulled apart the car, but it wasn't there. And I said, "Oh no, we must've left it behind when I took a poop." And she said, "No, Matt, you left it behind when you took a poop." "And I remember it has to be there. And I remember there was this brief break in the trees and this incline up through a bramble patch. And then I went over a log and that's where it is. All I need to do is find a log in the forest. I can go back and get it, I promise."

And she said, "No, Matt, no it's getting late. And our friends have things to do. We need to go home." But from the back seat, they're like, "Man, if you think you can get it, you should go for it." But I know what you're thinking. This sounds selfish to be like, I'm going to put my needs for redemption over the actual needs of my friends. But not only would she still be mad at me, I would forever be known in that family as the guy that lost her dad's knife taking a poop in the woods. We couldn't have that happen.

So we drove the hour back up the meandering mountain road. "So just for my own edification, does anyone have any more detailed memories about where I pooped in the woods? No? No. Okay. You can just say no. Okay, fine. Sorry." And we pulled into the trailhead and we saw the sun setting over the ancient Appalachians. And this time it wasn't something to marvel at, but a ticking time bomb reminding me of the task at hand. So I did the only thing I could do. I ran. The rhythm of my feet, my breath, and my heart fell in together and melded together the rhythms of my life, keeping my body alive. And I thought just about how alive I am. Every time my lungs burned and every time my feet felt like stones too heavy to pick up again.

By the time dusk was encroaching on us, I'd reached the dry riverbed. And in my remembrance, I had gone too far. So I pulled out my little flashlight, and it blinked to life. And I started scanning back along the trail. And as I went up, I found a little breach in the trees, and I pushed my way up *[motions clearing]* through the bramble patch and over the log, and I dug at the crack to see if it was the right spot. And it was definitely the right spot. But there was no knife. So I dug at the leaves *[acts out digging]* and I picked up the log and threw it aside, and I would tear apart the earth with my bare hands… bear.

And then I saw it. I picked it up and it *[picks up imaginary object]* was just a knife-shaped piece of black charcoal. It was dark. I failed. I did my best, and I'm just alone in the woods in the middle of the night, exhausted with nothing to show for it. I did my best and I failed. So I admitted a defeat.

I stumbled back through the bramble patch *[takes big step]* and down towards the trail. And there it was, just sitting up on the leaves, like some power greater than myself was looking at me and saying, "I got your back." But I didn't have time for that. So I picked it up and put it in my pocket because I had five miles back to run.

Need to remind you that in the dark, all by yourself, everything is a bear. I rode that primal fear all the way. My whole world became that little circle of light as I ran down the path. And as I was running, I heard this like *[grrrr]* and I kept running. I don't have time for this. *[grrrrrr]* sound. I was like, "Oh God." It sounded like, "Matt!" Was that Megan? Matt! Megan! And I ran off the path, and all three of them had come up the trails. From their perspective, I've just been alone in the woods for an hour and a half. And in the dark with a bear.

And I walked up to her and looked her right in the eyes. I said, "Megan, I didn't find your dad's knife. But I went to the knife store *[pulls imaginary knife from pocket]*." She hit me in the chest. And her gray-blue eyes caught the starlight. And I'm going to save the rest of this story for me.

4 "All of This Life, Right Out in Front of Us": Identifying Successful Story Structures

Evan and I were struggling. He had a general idea for a story: a camping trip with his friends that went bad when they were caught in the rain with a leaky tent. Evan is a funny, charming guy, but charm can only go so far. "What is this story about? Where is the conflict?" I kept asking him. Most of us have heard that, by definition, all stories must have conflict and rising action. Some people would say that a story with no conflict is not a story at all. Was the conflict here some half-baked version of "man versus nature"? I tried to help Evan manufacture conflict in the story, but it felt false because it just wasn't true. Poor Evan tried several directions with the story, but none of them seemed to result in the kind of dramatic arch that we were searching for. I worried we would never find a way into the story. So, we started over at the beginning. I asked Evan to recount the events of the trip and, as it turned out, there was much more there than the leaky tent. He and his pals had gone on these road trips before and, since they were getting older, this felt like this would be the last one. They goofed around on the beach, improvising characters they called The Camp Bandits—campers who'd gone feral out on the island. They marveled at the sea animals and the sunset, and they reveled in each other's company. There was, as he put it, "all this life out there in front of us." We mapped out these events in little chapters and Evan took that map for home to work. The resulting story clearly laid out the events of the trip in beautiful, hilarious detail that affirmed the importance of friendship. I didn't realize it at the time, but Evan's conflict-free structure might have been best described by the Kishōtenketsu model, which we will discuss in this chapter. It turned out to be a heartfelt and entertaining story, even in the absence of traditional conflict.

As this chapter will demonstrate, most of the time, stories do have conflict within them, although that conflict may reside inside the storyteller rather than crackling between characters. But that is not necessarily what makes a story a story. The assumption that all stories need to have two opposing figures wrestling in conflict toward a satisfying resolution has its roots in Greek drama. Drama, as a genre of literature, thrives on conflict, but drama is not the only literary genre. Poetry, for example, paints beautiful pictures that reflect important features of our lives without casting opposing forces against

DOI: 10.4324/9781003039266-4

each other. Storytelling is often more like prose fiction, offering a close look at the inner life of a particular person. Great stories often include conflict and have a dramatic arch, but they also offer vivid description and a unique point of view. We'll begin by looking at some typical story structures, most of which reflect the dramatic arch, whether they have conflict or not. Then we'll spend some time talking about rhetorical devices that work to help you structure your story. Next, we'll discuss how to determine what to leave in and what to leave out of a story as you structure it. Finally, we'll talk about the importance of devices for opening and closing stories to give them a sense of invitation and finality.

Common Story Structures

Before we get into specific story structures, it is important to reiterate that most of the ideas in this book are guidelines that you can converge with or diverge from as you feel is appropriate. Taking this attitude toward storytelling allows your unique perspective and inventiveness to come through, which is one of the main currencies of storytelling. With that in mind, these story structures are tried and true models that have worked across time and context. When a story does not work, it is often because of a structural problem. Like architecture, story structure ensures that your story will hold together under the pressure of a public presentation.

In its most basic form, the dramatic arch of a story follows a protagonist through a series of escalating events that change that person in some way. The nature of those escalating events and the shape of the curve may vary, but, in general, stories move forward, with rising complication and intensity, until they come back down in some kind of resolution. In this model, stories begin with the status quo, with things as they normally are. Next, some catalyst is introduced that ignites change in the status quo. The implications of that change usually escalate until they are resolved. The result is either a return to the status quo or, more likely, a new status quo that leaves the protagonist changed. In what follows, we'll discuss the Hollywood Structure, the Hero's Journey, and the classic Series of Unfortunate Events before examining a four-act conflict-free structure called Kishōtenketsu.

Hollywood Structure

Screenwriter Bill Idelson famously articulated what he aptly called the Hollywood Structure. In this format, the protagonist has a very specific goal, and there are obstacles to achieving that goal. There may be twists and turns along the way, and the protagonist usually gets help from supporting characters, but in the end, the hero achieves the goal. Luppa and Borst add to this structure, arguing that the hero often has a flaw or weakness that makes the obstacle particularly hard to overcome; thus, to attain the goal, the personal flaw must be overcome. We can imagine, for instance, a romantic comedy about a shy teenager who wants to ask a popular girl out to the big dance. He has to overcome his shyness, and any number of other social obstacles to achieve his goal. This is also often the case in action films, where the hero has a particular goal, usually saving the day, and a series of escalating obstacles are put in front of him.

It is important to note that the Hollywood Structure places the protagonist of the story squarely at the center of everything and can define the goal solely by its relationship to the protagonist. This is probably fine if the goal is to find the secret code that will save the world from nuclear annihilation by a sinister bad guy. It is more problematic if the goal is another person—as is often the case in many romantic comedies that focus on men pursuing women. When we describe someone as "the object of my affection," we're still describing them as an object. As we'll discuss later in this chapter, it is usually necessary to boil characters in your story down to their essence for the sake of clarity. There is a fine line between showing someone's essence and essentializing them. This does not mean that you should not tell stories about pursuing another person, but it does mean that you should be thoughtful about what ideology you are reiterating when you do so.

It is interesting to note that in television storytelling, as opposed to film, the protagonist usually returns to the status quo after experiencing the rising action of a particular episode. While narrative films are usually self-contained, television continues episode-to-episode, week-to-week. Radically altering the protagonist in each episode by introducing a new status quo would risk dismantling the formula that makes the show popular. When television shows do allow events to alter their characters, it usually happens over the course of several episodes, along a longer arch.

The Hero's Journey

In his book *The Hero with a Thousand Faces*, scholar Joseph Campbell describes the monomyth, or the hero's journey. In short, Campbell argued that a similar story pattern could be found in heroic myths across multiple contexts and generations. Filmmaker George Lucas famously drew on Campbell's work when creating the film *Star Wars*. We won't examine each of the seventeen specific steps of the hero's journey that Campbell lays out. Instead, we'll focus on the three broad steps: departure, initiation, and return. As the name suggests, Campbell's model focuses on a journey, so the first step is departure. A seemingly normal person is called to leave the comfortable confines of their familiar surroundings to travel into the unknown. In the second phase, initiation, the hero faces a series of trials that help transform the hero into the figure they will become. In the final stage, the return, the hero gestures to or returns to the site of the beginning of the story, underscore the changes that have taken place in the course of the story. Campbell's model is meant to make sense of common themes in mythology and, as was the case in *Star Wars*, can be used as a model for new stories.

Daniel, who we first met while he was preparing a story about breaking into his high school, created another story about his desire to mimic his literary hero, Huck Finn. Daniel's story begins when he is a younger child. After encountering Mark Twain's book, *Huckleberry Finn*, Daniel feels a call to adventure, after a fashion. He carefully planned to run away from home, with his dad helping to map out the route. He abandoned the plan, realizing he was too young to head out on the road alone and that he would miss his mother's cooking. But the desire to mimic Huck's adventure stuck with him. As a teenager, Daniel often headed out to a pond in a pasture near his house. On one particular day, he retreated to the pond to consider the story of Huck and Jim, which he had just re-read with his more grown-up eyes. He was contemplating the powerful depiction of slavery that he hadn't noticed as a child but weighed heavy on his teenage mind. He was jolted out of his contemplation by the sound of faraway gunshots. In the spirit of adventure, Daniel followed the sounds. He climbed high up in a tall tree and saw a few adults firing what appeared to be automatic weapons into an old, abandoned truck. Fear overtook Daniel, he scrambled down the tree and raced across the pasture, and hopped the fence, where he was confronted by a police officer. The officer asks if he's seen anything suspicious, and Daniel simply points back toward the gunshots and runs away. Arriving back home, he becomes aware of the comfort—and privilege—his home represents. He recognizes that he had the privilege to ignore Jim's plight in the original story. He recognizes that his interaction with the police officer might have gone very differently if he wasn't white, male, and visibly middle-class. Upon his return home, he is brought to a new consciousness.

Daniel's story does not precisely mirror Campbell's monomyth. It does, however, gesture to the broad strokes of the hero's journey: leaving the safe confines of the familiar, facing trials, and coming home changed. It's not important for Daniel to try and wedge his story into Campbell's framework. Rather, models like the hero's journey offer storytellers like Daniel a point of departure, a springboard, from which to begin crafting their own stories.

Campbell's work has been, perhaps rightly, criticized for its emphasis on Western myths and male protagonists. Others point out Campbell's tendency to emphasize details that support his thesis while ignoring information that undermines his work. Campbell's work can, however, offer a useful stepping off point for storytellers who want to tell a story that is structured as a journey without religiously adhering to—and perhaps even subverting—the hero's journey structure.

Kishōtenketsu

Many stories based on our lived experience can easily fit into a four-act conflict-free structure called Kishōtenketsu. This structure appears, for example, in Japanese manga, Chinese poetry, and a variety of other storytelling mediums. Kishōtenketsu is a Japanese word composed of four characters that each represent part of the structure. The first *ki*, represents the introduction of the setting, characters, and other information needed to understand the story. In the second act, represented by the character *sho*, we learn more about the characters and their relationships with each other and the world around them. As I will say often in this book, there are no hard and fast rules in storytelling, but if there were one, it would probably be this: the audience must care about the people in a story for the story to work. In the third act, represented by the character *ten*, the story becomes more complicated. That does not mean there is a traditional conflict per se, but an unexpected twist occurs. This twist may seem unrelated to the previous events, though they do tie together in the end. The final stage, *ketsu*, offers reconciliation as we discover the effect the complications had on what we learned in acts one, two, and three.

Although I didn't know it at the time, Evan's story, mentioned at the start of this chapter, followed the Kishōtenketsu model. We meet the characters and learn the circumstances. With the characters and circumstances established, Evan goes to develop the characters. This happens as they explore the island and as Evan reenacts their Camp Bandit hijinks. The twist comes when their fun is interrupted by a rainstorm that they nonetheless make it through. As we leave Evan and his friends at the end of the story, they are not fundamentally changed. Instead, they have passed through one last fun and thoughtful trip together as they face adulthood on the horizon.

Revelation

Like the Kishōtenketsu structure, a revelation-focused structure is less about conflict and more about making a series of events visible, revealing one after the other. There may be tension inside these revelations, but there is often no conflict or even rising action per se. Rather, a series of events (and the emotions that go along with them) are revealed in an interesting and artful way.

Mace (who uses they/them pronouns) created a beautiful story (which appears in whole later in this book) that lent itself to this structure. Their story tacked back and forth in time between a party where their queer identity was celebrated in the present and their struggles with identity in the past. It begins with Mace revealing they'd been invited to a party by an old friend, continues as Mace expresses anxiety about going to the party, next flashing back to high school, where they never felt comfortable in their own skin, only to finally find acceptance at the party. If there is any conflict in this story, it is probably best understood as Mace's conflict with self-definition and social expectations. It would be fair to say the story doesn't rise to a "peak" of any kind but rather simply and cleverly reveals a series of events. Any notion of tension or conflict takes a backseat to the slow unfolding of Mace's self-realization and acceptance. There is a sense of catharsis at the end of the story, but it is framed as a momentary resolution, with Mace making peace with the fact that they are still waiting for more to be revealed about who they are. We'll meet Mace again in Chapter 7, when we discuss embodiment.

The close relative of the revelation structure is the "series of unfortunate events." This structure maps episodes in a story where things get increasingly worse as the story goes on. Each episode crashes into the next, and things just get worse, and worse for the protagonist. We've all had days like this: in the morning, you realize your car is low on gas, you get gas and spill it on your clothes, you arrive late to work, and you discover you're late for a meeting you forgot about. You arrive at the meeting unprepared, out of breath, and smelling like gasoline. Judith Viorst and Ray Cruz's beloved children's book *Alexander and the Terrible, Horrible, No Good, Very Bad Day* comes to mind as an example of the kind of cascading problems individuals face in their everyday lives. These events are mortifying when they happen, which is exactly what makes them funny and interesting in hindsight.

Like other stories, a story structured around a series of unfortunate events begins with a protagonist, usually in normal conditions. The unfortunate events begin with small events that turn into larger events and get more and more dramatic as the story goes on. It is important that the event with the highest stakes come last in the series. A small irritation arriving after a cataclysmic event blunts the impact of that event. Think back of the previous example about getting gas on your clothes and being unprepared for a meeting. Imagine that story culminating in losing your job, thus cutting off your income and stifling your career goals. After you leave work, another driver cuts you off in traffic. This would be another unfortunate event, but is it really worse than losing your job? Probably not. It is hard to make the traffic mishap seem important after a much more serious event has taken place. Kyle typified this structure with a story we called "First Worst" about his first time taking a date to a school dance. He dressed all wrong, he ordered too much food, and he ignored his date to play games. Basically, he made all the mistakes you can imagine. The unfolding revelation of his mistakes offered a relatable look at his youthful obliviousness.

Mosaic

The word *mosaic* usually refers to laying small pieces of material—stone, paper, fabric, and so forth—together in a deliberate fashion to create a picture or design. When used as a metaphor for story structure, mosaic can refer to setting various short scenes or vignettes that ultimately come together to create a whole picture of the story. This structure stands in contrast to structures where events proceed in a chronological order, with one action leading to the next. We'll discuss Ben's story in greater detail in Chapter 8, but in short, Ben created a moving story about a close friend who committed suicide at a young age. The two boys had participated in Boy Scouts together, and Ben structured his story through a series of vignettes: about Scouting with his friend, his friend's death, and the grief experienced in the aftermath. What is interesting about the use of these vignettes is that they appear out of order in time and do not, in some cases, naturally lead to one another. Ben found artful ways to transition from one idea to another, even when those ideas moved around in temporal and narrative order. The resulting story is not at all hard to follow and paints a vivid picture of the events. I think, perhaps, Ben did this because no one stopped him and it simply made sense to him. I honestly marvel at what is possible when we set ideas next to each other and trust the audience to put the pieces together.

Narrative Braiding

A narrative braid structure weaves two or more narrative threads together, wrapping them around each other to highlight the metaphorical relationship between the two narratives. In essence, two stories are being told alongside each other, and each story enhances the other. For example, David created a beautiful story about his trouble communicating with his father, wrapped around a composite narrative that mirrored the typical structure of a Godzilla movie. David and his father bonded over classic Godzilla films, and he saw a parallel between his struggles with his dad and Godzilla's struggles with human beings. Jovan created a folklore-inspired story about an ethereal creature piercing the veil between the magical world and the human world and paralleled that story with the true story of his mother's pregnancy and his birth. As mentioned previously, Gal wove his own experiences navigating middle school as a very big kid with wrestler Andre the Giant's experiences navigating the world as a giant. In all these examples, both narrative threads have their own arch and resolution—often coming together artfully at the end.

The mosaic structure and narrative braiding both incorporate juxtaposition to enhance meaning. One could argue that all meaning is the product of juxtaposition: one image or idea set in relationship or contrast with another. This is, of course, how we compose words, by setting letters next to each other to create sound and meaning. The juxtaposition of one narrative with another gives both narratives a greater sense of depth and texture. The mosaic structure allows us to see events in the same story in relation to one another, apart from the order in which they took place in space and time. In both cases, the audience can easily become an active participant as they try to make sense of the narrative pieces and threads.

The structures offered here are not the only structures available to you as a storyteller. However, they do offer a look at some of the most common structures. Your story may follow one of these models closely, borrow from several models, or depart from them entirely. In the end, the effectiveness of your structure is determined by the audience and whether or not they find it sensible and useful. While that is true, most western audiences come preloaded with expectations that match these models. As such, it is worthwhile to at least understand them.

Structuring Devices

When structuring your story, you may want to utilize structuring devices. These structuring devices are repeated turns of phrase that act like signposts to help the audience remain clear about where the story is going. For example, in Matt's story about losing a knife in the woods, he repeats the simple phrase, "but time keeps on ticking," to signal that time is passing. In her story about her hero, comedian Gilda Radner, Ella borrowed a structuring device from a documentary about Radner called *Dear Gilda*. Ella started several parts of the story with the phrase, "Dear Gilda," as if she were writing her hero a letter and addressing her in the first person. It was a charming way to transition between parts of the story. In Kyle's story about a terrible first date mentioned earlier, he enumerated each mistake, beginning with the first one– "This would be known as mistake number one" he announced as he described his first misstep. With each mistake, he returned to this enumeration. This strategy underlined his cascading errors throughout the night. It is important to remember that audiences who are listening to, rather than reading, a story need structure to keep the story straight in their minds. Turns of phrase like the ones described here give the audience something to hang on to as they listen.

Determining What to Include and Exclude

Human beings access the world through our senses, which are housed in our bodies. Personal storytelling is, in some ways, a recounting of what the body has experienced and what the senses have taken in. For better or worse, our sensory and embodied experiences happen in great excess to our ability of process and express them. Imagine, for example, walking through a busy cafeteria. People are moving all around you, people are talking and laughing at tables, dozens of smells intermingle, the coffee maker squeaks and steams somewhere behind you, music plays from speakers in the ceiling, and your own thoughts compete for your attention. As you snake through the cafeteria, you're probably barely conscious of all these things happening around you, but your internal operating system keeps you moving successfully toward your meal. Your senses have chosen to shut out some information and move other information to the foreground. Storytelling is like that: we zoom in on some aspects of a story and exclude others.

Telling stories about your own experience can make it difficult to decide what to include and what to exclude. Sometimes, all the details in our stories feel important because they are part of our lives and include the people that we love. However, choices must be made to make your particular story work for an audience. It is useful for every story to have what I call a North Star. The North Star, of course, refers to the star Polaris, which famously stays stationary and bright, making it useful for navigation. The North Star of a story is the central purpose of a story. When faced with decisions about what to include and what to exclude in a story, one can look to their North Star and ask, "does that this part of the story work to support the central purpose of the story?" If the answer to that question is "no" then that part of the story probably does not need to be included. Having a North Star for your story can take the decision out of your hands, making it easier to leave out things that feel important to you but are not important to the story. For example, think back to Ben's story about his friend and Scouting mentioned earlier in this Chapter. While composing that story, Ben originally included an anecdote about games his Scout Troupe would play while hiking. It was a fun little bit, and Ben liked telling that part of the story, but we found that the story was too long and dragged in the middle. Ultimately, we had to ask ourselves: does this part of the story really serve the goal we have in mind? It turned out that fun little bit drew the story away from its purpose, and so Ben cut it out. By staying true to the North Star of his story, Ben was able to make the right choice about what to leave in and what to leave out.

Rhetorical scholar Kenneth Burke offers another model for thinking about what to include and what to exclude. Burke introduced the phrase "terministic screens" (44) to describe the ways that we pick and choose language, or terminology, to direct other people (and ourselves) toward particular interpretations and away from other interpretations. The inclusion of certain language can highlight something. Choosing to not include some information directs us away from thinking about that information. Burke would tell us that language is never a perfect reflection of reality, but even when it comes close to reflecting reality, speakers still select some content and deflect other content in the process of describing the world. Sometimes these choices are reflected simply in how a storyteller describes someone or something. Other times, these decisions are central to the process of structuring your story.

For example, imagine you are telling a story about preparing for and going out on a big date. You're nervous about what might happen, but after a few mishaps, things end up working out and a romance blossoms. Now imagine that this story takes place right after your brother was in an accident, leaving him unable to walk for a few weeks. That event might have been a big part of your life at the time, but it probably has nothing to do with the date you're going on. Including that information in the story might distract from the central purpose of the story. Alternatively, imagine that this big date story takes place shortly after your parents announced they are getting a divorce. That event would surely seem important in your life and, on the surface, might not have anything to do with the date. However, you might imagine a way to tell both stories parallel to one another, contrasting your parent's breakup with your new romance or suggesting that their divorce is feeding your anxiety about the date. This information may add a richer texture to the story, while the detail about your brother's accident would likely seem superfluous. This is just one example of the kinds of decisions you must make when structuring a story.

Not only must you decide what events to include and exclude, but you must also decide what to tell the audience about people who appear in the story. Again, this can be tricky when you are telling a story about yourself because the people in the story might be very important to you. It may feel wrong to reduce those three-dimensional people who occupy your life into two-dimensional characters in a story. But if you're careful, you can capture their essence without overloading your story with details you don't need.

You can use a variety of performative and rhetorical approaches to capture the essence of the people in your story. I worked with Molly on more than one story where she battled with her mother. Each time her mom appeared to speak in a story, Molly would adopt a relaxed, leaned-back posture, and pantomime her mother holding a wine glass. Molly would mimic her mother and look down her nose while she scolded her daughter (who was the very person telling the story!). Molly's mother is a lovely, multifaceted person. She likes wine, but also likes many other things. But for the purposes of this story, Molly adopted a performative approach that captured the essence of her mother that was appropriate for a story where they were having conflict. Alternatively, concise and descriptive language can tell us what we need to know about one of the people in your story. For example, Sarah introduced her brother into a story where his mischief was going to play an important role in the climatic moment. She describes him as a kind of mad scientist, going to on describe a time he called his friend on the phone and then baked the receiver in the microwave just to find out what it sounded like. Sarah loves her brother, but this concise little anecdote captured the mischievous part of his personality that figured so importantly into the story. There are a variety of ways to portray the people in your story, the key is to figure out what the audience really needs to know about those people and focus on that.

Opening and Closing Stories

Many people struggle with the question: where should I begin my story? As with most problems you face in the story-making process, the real question is: what do I want this part of my story to accomplish? For the most part, the beginning of any story should draw the audience in and spark their interest. In what follows, we'll look at a few useful strategies for doing that, but first we'll look at some common, yet unsuccessful, strategies people use.

First, many people start their stories with exposition that includes facts: the date, the season, and their age at the time. It sounds something like this: "So, a few years ago when I was 14 or 15 years old, we lived a brick house, but then we moved to an apartment. When we lived in the apartment …" Not only are these facts nonspecific, but they are also not interesting, and they are not necessary to know at the outset of the story. These kinds of facts often reveal themselves naturally as they are woven into the fabric of the narrative. This may be information we need to know, but information is not what gets an audience invested in a story.

Next, many people start their stories by revealing what happens at the end and explaining the moral or theme before the story even begins. It sounds something like this: "You never know what unexpected things life will throw at you, but if you persevere, you can handle life's curve balls." Whatever story follows, we now know that the story will include surprises, and everything will be fine in the end. We're not allowed to discover this for ourselves and any suspense that might have existed has been defused. Later, we'll talk about starting *in media res*, but this is not that. This means giving away what happens in the story before it even starts. Neither beginning with exposition nor beginning by revealing the theme of the story does much to ignite the imagination of an audience. Luckily, there are some tried and true methods of raising the audience's interest in a story.

The phrase I mentioned earlier, *in media res*, is Latin and literally means "in the middle of things." Beginning a story with action, somewhere in the middle of the narrative, and then jumping back to the chronological beginning of the story can be an effective way to elicit interest in the audience. Beginning *in media res* has several benefits. First, it usually means that you are beginning with action rather than exposition. Action tends to hook an audience and lead them on with the promise of more excitement. Second, beginning in the middle of the narrative tends to raise questions for the audience that the story can answer later. Raising questions keeps the audience wondering what will happen next and invested in co-creating the experience.

Chris' story offers an excellent example of beginning in the middle of things. He began his story with a vivid description of himself sitting on a bench in a police station. He narrates his racing mind as he eyes the gun on the hip of a nearby police officer. He feels guilty. He feels afraid. He is too young to go to jail. He is 7 years old. The audience laughs at the reveal of this final piece of information, and Chris gives them a sly smile. Then he jumps back to the chronological beginning of the story and explains that he'd followed some older boys who were throwing rocks at a train. When the police arrived to stop them, the older boys ran off, leaving little Chris to get picked up. But before the audience learns any of this, they are left asking the question: how did this little kid wind up in a police station? They want to know more, and they are invested in the story.

A second strategy is to begin with an intriguing or provocative statement. This approach requires some thought and cleverness but yields good results. There are any number of possibilities for clever remarks, but the intention is always the same. These crisp opening lines are meant to jolt the audience, raise questions, and signal that the story and the storyteller are going to be interesting. Josiah began one of his stories by stating (with just a hint of exasperation): "It's not easy being the smartest person in your family." Connor began a story about visiting his Rabbi with visible irritation as he quipped, "You know what really pisses me off about Noah and the Ark?" Surprised laughter filled the space that followed. Harper started a story about her grandfather with the provocative and confrontational assertion, "My family loves Christmas more than yours." Josiah began another one of his stories by saying, "Think like an adult. My parents told me this all the time." I could go on, but you can begin to see how these kinds of provocative and intriguing statements can draw an audience in.

A third strategy for beginning a story is to begin with action. By "action" I mean some sort of physical, gestural, or aural act that captures the attention of an audience. We'll discuss physicality later on in this book, but often this action takes the form of pantomime that helps to draw the world of the story before the audience's imagination. For instance, Jimmy began a story leaning over a bit, arms behind his back, and blowing air out of his mouth. He followed this action by saying, "Wow. I made it. 10 years old," and we immediately understand he's been blowing out candles on a birthday cake. Thomas began a story with his back to the audience and whistling a tune that sounded like an alarm before reaching over and batting at an invisible alarm clock. Troy began a story with his face down before raising his head, blinking, rubbing his eyes, and looking around with a dazed look on his face. "I woke up," Troy said, "in the passenger seat of an RV." These are just a few examples of the ways that action can start a story and gain attention.

Sometimes it is best to start with a simple, vivid description. Recalling that storytelling is an effort to get an audience to see, think, and feel the same thing at the same time, vivid description speaks right to that desire. Mace began one of their stories with an air of authority, saying,

> I am seven feet tall. Seven foot three if you count my platform heals. I am a god, and no one can escape my gaze. The blue neon light flickers behind me, it draws my silhouette in time with the growing suspense. The squishing, sticking sound of the floor echos off the wall in this musty back hallway as I slowly step forward. I was wronged tonight but now, now I am a god!

Mace's vivid description defies what we know to be true. We can see them and know they are not seven feet tall. But the neon light, the sticky floor, and the musty hallway all strongly evoke the imagery that Mace is trying to place squarely in the minds of the audience. Mace is also, in this case, beginning in media res at the peak of the story. They are also using hyperbole to enhance the humor and making provocative statements ("I am seven feet" and "I am a god") to draw our attention. This is a wonderful example of combining multiple strategies at once.

It does not feel good to end a story and hear silence followed by scattered applause. When you hear that, it usually means that the end of your story caught the audience off guard; they weren't sure you were finished, and they were unprepared to clap. The end of a story most often resolves the central tension of the story. The resolution of the central tension of a story is often referred to as catharsis. In what follows, we'll look at the idea of catharsis, when catharsis may not be necessary, and creating a so-called "button" to bring your story to a tidy end.

Catharsis is a Greek word that means, in most translations, a kind of purification or cleansing. In the context of storytelling, catharsis refers to the resolution of tension produced in a story. I like the idea of describing the resolution of tension as a purging or a cleansing—as a release that wipes away the anxiety the story has produced. It underlines the fact that the story, and the journey it has taken us on, is coming to a close. Storytelling is a funny thing: audiences have been exposed to stories since childhood, and they know, for the most part, catharsis is coming at the end of every story. And yet, audiences get swept up in stories and feel the tension of stories in their imaginations and bodies. They hold on through the journey of the story, waiting for the release that they know will come. Catharsis comes in many forms. Sometimes it is produced when one of the two competing forces in a story wins out. Think about Matt's story about losing a precious knife in Chapter 3. When, against all odds, Matt finds the knife in the woods, the tension in the story is released. It was washed away, and the audience, and Matt, can breathe easy again. In other cases, catharsis is produced when the storyteller demonstrates that they have come out okay on the other side of the story.

Occasionally, you will find yourself telling a story about an experience that has not resolved or is unresolvable. In Chapter 3, we looked at a student's story about his foster brothers leaving his family. At various points in the composition process, he tried to provide closure for the audience, some sort of catharsis. He composed a couple different endings for the story, each focused on offering the audience some kind of moral or lesson for their lives. However, with each attempt, it seemed as if the moral he was offering was meant to supersede the particular heartbreaking circumstances of his brothers leaving. After much deliberation, we decided to end the story with no button and no catharsis. He kisses his brothers goodbye one last time and closes the door on his way back to school—not knowing when he'll see them again. The effect is that the audience is left a little breathless and feeling an echo of the loss he felt that day. In short, after he leaves his brothers, there is nowhere else for the story to go. It doesn't get any more emotionally potent than that moment, so that is where he ended it. This example describes a very specific situation but illustrates the fact that conventional wisdom—that all stories need catharsis—is not always correct.

Once you've decided how to deal with the catharsis at the end of a story, it is time to start searching for a button for your story. A *button* refers to a clever, pithy statement that completes the story. It is so named because it snaps the story shut and brings it to a tidy finish. The search for a good button is an art, not a science. It is a matter of finding the right combination of words and sentiment that brings the story to a natural end. It is best to approach the search for just the right phrase as a game you are playing with yourself. Keep trying different phrases out loud until you find the one that strikes you.

Courtney told a hilarious story about her last day working at a pizza place called Pizza and Beyond. She repeated the name of the restaurant a few times in the story, to great comic effect. In the story, the restaurant had a loose relationship with health codes and professional protocol. She offered a few anecdotes that illustrated this fact. But the true nature of Pizza and Beyond was made vividly clear to her one day when she sliced the tip of her finger off while chopping vegetables for a salad. As she tended to her wound, she turned to see the salad she was making go out the door to be delivered—with the tip of her finger alongside the tomatoes and cumbers. As the story concluded, Courtney explained that she realized she deserved to work at a better place than this, and she got a better job at a better restaurant. "But," Courtney concluded, "I feel like I left a little piece of myself behind at Pizza and Beyond." The double meaning was immediately clear to the audience, bringing a hilarious ending to what was already a funny story. Courtney's clever word play offers one example of how a button can be memorable and meaningful.

This chapter has focused on the ways that one might think about the structure of a story. You'll notice that at no point yet have I encouraged you to write anything. Thus far, our discussion of structure has been conceptual. In Chapter 5, we will begin discussing how to put these concepts into practice and apply them to the stories you want to tell.

Questions to Consider

1 Choose one of your story ideas and try to map it with three of the story structures mentioned in this chapter. Which one works best? Why does it work better than others?
2 Brainstorm your own list of examples that illustrate these narrative structures. Which ones do you find most appealing?
3 Read David's story at the end of this chapter. What strategies does he use to make the Godzilla part of the story vivid in the mind's eye?

"Deep Ocean"
Created and Performed by David Reese

About 70% of the earth is covered in water. Nearly 2% is in lakes and rivers. Around 5% is caught in glaciers. That means that 63% of the earth is covered in ocean. As humans, we have explored 5–7% of the ocean floor. We have explored less than half a percent of the ocean itself. In the deep ocean, that percentage is even smaller.

But even though human eyes have not gazed upon its contents, the ocean still rumbles. Creatures move and stir, *[Hands moving like water]* water crashes and churns. Waves pound the shore, and the moonlight is out on the surface. Scale by scale, hundred feet by hundred feet of creature fill the night sky, roar! It's Godzilla! *[Looks up]* Godzilla versus King Gidra, Godzilla versus Mecha Godzilla, and Godzilla versus Mothra. I was in a Blockbuster.

For those of you two young to remember Blockbuster, it's like a Redbox but a whole store. Instead of DVDs, they had these things called VHS tapes, and they're rectangles with film in it ... Google it. Godzilla is amazing, lizards are cool, but giant space monster nuclear lizards, yeah.

Of course I never meant to rent any of the movies because my father had every Godzilla movie that touched cable recorded at home, but at

Blockbuster I got to look at the covers. I looked up and saw my father standing by the door, reading a paperback science fiction novel. Now my father is always reading a paperback science fiction novel, at work, eating, sleeping, and driving. But standing close to the door was his sign that it was time to go.

Rubble lay strewn across the streets as people ran terrified in every direction. A giant shadow blocks out the sun as a pterodactyl-like creature screeches and dives at its prey. The people fade out as the camera zooms in on a pile of pterodactyl poop the size of a Honda Civic. And on top, the glasses of a now very deceased scientist. Because apparently pterodactyl stomachs do not digest glasses well.

My father is the kind of guy who will wear the same style of glasses, hair cut, flannel shirt, and Converse shoes for three decades. Three decades. In a similar streak with a large green recliner he sat in. Now this green recliner is the same color as the car he purchased, the winter coat he still wears, and the suit he got married in. When my father finds something he likes, he sticks to it.

Of course, next to the chair were boxes and piles of Legos, which is where I sat, and together we watched hours of cinematic brilliance. By this, I mean the Godzilla material created in Japan from 1954 to 1995. There's a particular American movie made in 1998 called Godzilla with a tag line: Size Does Matter. It is not canon, and it's dead to me. My love for Godzilla was matched by my father's enthusiasm for science fiction and all things monster, and I think that made it easier to communicate with a 10-year-old, which is hard for someone with a logical mind.

Godzilla tramped and trudged through the city with no regard for human life, *[stomps feet]* crushing cars and people alike. Gritty dust clogged the lungs of citizens, who couldn't scream through the coughing. Tanks came around the corner and thud, thud, Godzilla was pounded with shells and rockets, and he let out another, "Roar!" Not of rage, but of fear. Godzilla was misplaced. Nuclear tests drew him out of the ocean, and then now he was in a foreign land, stepping across foreign territory and foreign objects, and all of a sudden he's being hit with bullets and explosions. He gained nothing. He just wanted to be somewhere safe. But there was no safe haven to be found.

Middle school is hard. I think that's a sentiment that a lot of people share, but for me especially, I was troubled. Not like *beat the kid up next to me* trouble, but like the *kid next to me beat me up* kind of trouble. That, combined with the usual academic pressures, means I didn't do so well, and I hid my assignments in my closets, because that's how you fix your grades.

My father is a structural and forensic engineer. This means his job basically has three parts. One, find a building's structural fault. Two, design a solution to the building's structural fault. And three, execute the solution. He's really good at it, and it always works. He did this with buildings, and with his son. I had a fault, my grades. The solution is to remove all distractions. The execution, remove the one thing that kept this child afloat in the purgatory of middle school, video games. I can feel the judgment from here; they may not have been important to you, but they are damn important to me, and it sucked.

It didn't work. It didn't work, so Mothra slammed Godzilla against the mountain again. As he fell down to ground level, Mothra came over the top and let out another painful dosage of dust in Godzilla's eyes, and he let out another roar! Not of hatred, but of pain. Red blood oozed from his bark-like skin. Godzilla was far from anywhere he could call home, and there was no sign of an end to the torment. But the humans, Mothra and Godzilla, they all wanted the same thing: for Godzilla to be gone. But they had no way to communicate it. They didn't share a language.

The end of middle school was tense. I did all I could; I just wanted to get into the same advanced high school my brother did: Wheeler Magnet for Science and Math. It was like the MIT for high schools. If I did well enough I could go, I could be smart too.

Word came during CPR training with my father in the Boy Scouts. It was a yes. I got in, my test was enough, my grades were enough, for once I was enough. He turned to me and said one word: "Congratulations. You're in." Okay, three words, same sentiment. In engineering terms, a pillar of support was put where the tension was, and things were stable for now.

Mothra dropped a bleeding and broken Godzilla into the open ocean, and he crashed through the surface. Water surrounded the lizard, and as he descended, it grew dark and quiet. But now Godzilla was somewhere he knew, somewhere he could trust. And though Godzilla and the island were safe for now, the ocean still rumbles.

Years later, my father and I still didn't talk much, but sometimes you don't have to. And when Godzilla was rereleased in its original format with English subtitles in a local theater, my yes came quickly. We sat side-by-side and watched Godzilla let out a "Roar!" And it registered at the same frequency for both of us.

Isn't it fascinating how a creature that can tear the world asunder can bring two people closer together.

5 "Joey Owned Cats": Composing Stories from Action to Text

I liked Tyler right away. In a world full of people who are trying to impress each other, Tyler was always comfortable in his own skin. I encouraged him to join my storytelling class, and he patiently reminded me that he was not a performer—he liked other aspects of performance like building sets. I told him to join us anyway. Acting, I told him, is for the most part about disappearing into a character. Storytelling, on the other hand, is about making yourself appear before an audience. Tyler, like a lot of so-called "nonperformers," was very interesting when he was just being himself. We wound up working on a simple story about his childhood: the time Tyler followed his revered older brother Jeff and their neighbor, Joey, to a nearby creek to play. Tyler wound up being attacked by wasps, and his older brother saved him. The story was a tribute to his brother, who is still his hero to this day.

One day, as we were just starting to work, Tyler had not yet written anything down. He also seemed a little bit nervous. I encouraged him to just stand up and start talking. He began casually, saying, "Okay, okay, okay so…" I stopped him. "Let's just keep that as the opening," I told him. It's not particularly clever or enticing, but in that moment, as Tyler repeated himself, waving his hands a little dismissively, you immediately got a sense of who Tyler was. "You tell me this story is about your brother. What did you like about him so much as a kid?" I asked Tyler. He listed a few reasons: he was older, had a lot of friends, and a bunch of awesome *Jurassic Park* action figures. "They were dope" Tyler said. Okay, I said, let's keep all that too. Joey's character was not well fleshed out. He was in the story, but we couldn't see him. "Tell me three things about Joey," I asked Tyler. "Joey," he said, "was fine but he was one of those people you hang out with because they're your neighbor. Joey was the kind of kid who wore a helmet when he rode his bike, he watched his language. Joey owned cats." I burst out laughing at that last bit: Joey owned cats. If you know those three things about Joey, do you really need to know anything else? Joey may look a little different to every audience member, but they all could see him. That line still makes me laugh. At this point, Tyler was just talking, but he came up with some great pieces that we kept in the story. In the end, he composed the entire story out loud and never wrote anything down.

DOI: 10.4324/9781003039266-5

Until this point, we have been laying the groundwork for the discussion that happens in this chapter. This chapter offers a method for composing personal stories out loud, in rehearsal, before writing them down. I refer to this method as working from action to text. We'll begin by discussing why composing stories out loud is so useful. Next, we'll look at developing a story through conversation. Next, we'll pause to identify the central images in your story. With those images in mind, we'll discuss story mapping and what I call the "Six Big Beats." Finally, we'll look at a model for using all the material you've developed in a rehearsal process that brings the story to life.

Why Work from Action to Text?

What do we really mean when we work from action to text as opposed to beginning with text? The distinction is fairly simple. Most conventional theatre works from text to action. That is, most plays and musicals begin with a script that is staged by actors, a director, designers, a crew, and so forth. They begin with text—the script—and move toward action—the production of the play. Obviously, that's also how most movies and television are created too, and there is absolutely nothing wrong with that. Working from action to text, on the other hand, means beginning with speech, gesture, improvisational language, conversation, and imagining imagery and slowly building a fully formed performance that captures the product of that action. If, at the end of this process, you choose to write the story down, then I don't consider that final script a piece of literature, where the written form is in the foreground. Instead, I consider that final script a record of all the rehearsal and performance that preceded it, just as we can imagine a painting as the record of the brush strokes that created it. Working from action to text puts performance in the foreground. Pursuing this method can make stories easier to remember and give them the quality of speech, rather than the quality of writing.

First, it is simply easier to remember something you have composed out loud because, when you are composing out loud, you won't say something unnatural or out of character. The things we say spontaneously or that come out naturally usually reflect our true feelings. Speaking out loud allows our honest feelings to come through. This approach helps you get out of your head, so to speak, and into a more embodied mode of expression. The mind will sometimes deny what the body knows, and the mind likes to take the reins when it comes to writing. Mark Twain, an accomplished solo performer and live storyteller in his own right, famously quipped, "Always tell the truth—it's the easiest thing to remember." In this case, the "truth" is what honestly comes from your mouth and your memory, and that is indeed the easiest thing to remember. Later in this chapter, we'll discuss some mnemonic devices for organizing your ideas that help you remember the content of a story.

Second, composing a story out loud gives it the quality of speech rather than the quality of writing. Trying to write down our memories can create a level of literary mediation between what we feel and what we wind up putting down on the page. Or, in other words, writing can get in the way of expressing how we really feel. Many people grew up in an educational system that taught writing was something they were meant to aspire to, not something they did naturally. Essays and compositions were graded with red pens that told us we'd not met some standard that is not our own. I almost failed English my second year of high school because my style as a writer veered toward the surreal, and that did not fit my teacher's narrow definition of so-called good writing. What's more, even if you are comfortable writing, most writing *sounds* like writing. It tends to be precise and organized. It tends to sound formal. It doesn't sound like speech. People speak in incomplete sentences, they take parenthetical side trips inside of sentences, they bend the sounds of words for meaning, they intone sarcastically, they pause for effect, and they punctuate their remarks with facial expressions—all things we don't tend to do in writing but are essential for performance. Live speech tells us much more about the point of view of the author than writing, simply because the author's body is present in speech, and it is not present in writing. The sound, posture, and affect of the body can communicate information without having to say it explicitly. Interpreting all of these extra-textual and performative messages allows the audience to more fully contribute to the shared experience of meaning-making.

Composing a story out loud usually results in a product that feels conversational and authentic rather than deliberate and studied. This is true even when, in truth, the performance is deliberately planned. There is a word in Italian, *sprezzatura*, which describes an intentional casualness, meant to obscure the artfulness of something. Imagine, for example, a well-dressed Italian gentleman who stuffs a handkerchief in his pocket with the deliberate intent of making it look unintentional. Now imagine that concept in performance. As far back as 1915, actor William Gillette used the phrase, "the illusion of the first time," to describe the way actors create the impression that the words they are speaking are spontaneous rather than scripted. As a storyteller, you want to create your own illusion of the first time so that your story feels spontaneous and honest. That your audience knows your performance is carefully rehearsed is immaterial, they're willing to go along for the ride. This sort of studied and intentional casualness can best be achieved by first composing a story out loud, from action to text.

Step 1: Composing in Conversation

Storytelling does not require much in the way of props, costumes, or lighting, but, in this case, it does require a friend. The first step in developing a story out loud is telling it to a friend who does not already know the story. This works best if you stand on your feet and tell the story as it naturally falls out of your body. I have no biological or neurological explanation for why it works better to tell the story standing up on your feet, but I assure you it does work better. Perhaps this is because your body is slightly less relaxed and more engaged than it is when you are sitting. Perhaps standing tells your body, "Shape up, this is important!" Whatever the case, it is important that you stand up and tell your story to your friend. Let it fall out of your body in whatever order or form feels natural to you. Don't judge or censor yourself. I realize that is easier said than done. Consider this: every product that has ever been made—from motorcycles to movie scripts—went through R&D, the research and development process where choices were made, ideas were discarded, and concepts were allowed to grow. This is the start of the R&D stage of your story.

Before you begin telling your story, ask your friend to listen closely to your story and prepare to offer you some specific feedback. Specifically, ask them to listen for the following things:

1 What stood out the most in the story?
2 What, if anything, seemed superfluous?
3 What did they want to hear more about?
4 What questions did they have or what did they not understand?
5 What do they think your story is about? What is the theme?

Once you've stood up and told your story to your friend, chat with them about their answers to the questions above. Then, stand right back up and tell it again while attempting to incorporate their feedback. Remove anything superfluous. Amplify the things that stood out. Answer any questions they had. Try driving the story in the direction of the theme they identified. It is crucial that you stand right back after receiving your feedback. In fact, it is best not to sit down while listening to your feedback and simply start again from that standing position. However, you may want to take just a moment to jot down notes about the feedback you've been given. That said, the longer you stay standing, composing your story out loud in front of someone, the quicker your story will come together.

This step, receiving and incorporating feedback at the initial development stage, is important for at least three reasons. First, every time you repeat a story, its form will start to firm up in your mind. Repeating it one time and then another immediately after you finish speeds up the process of solidifying the story. Second, having an audience (even an audience of one trusted friend) will encourage you to explain things that might otherwise go left unsaid if you were only telling the story to yourself. When we are talking about our own experiences, we sometimes just assume that everything makes sense because it makes sense to us. Explaining characters, events, and actions to others adds more essential meat to the bones of the story. Third, and perhaps most importantly, this exercise gives you an initial sense of how another person hears your story. I recall hearing a student tell someone a story from their childhood that they thought was charming and funny. The person giving them feedback gently suggested that their story wasn't funny and, frankly, felt more like child neglect. The storyteller had no idea another person would hear the story that way. Remember, our goal is to get an audience to co-create the story with you while seeing it the way you want them to see it. Beginning by getting feedback from another person gets the process started.

Step 2: Identifying Images, Objects, Relationships, Setting, and Characters

Once you've gotten the story out of your body you can begin zooming in on what is important in the story. If you recall the very start of this book, I described the purpose of storytelling is to get a group of people to see, think, and feel the same thing at the same time. The next step in this process is determining what you want them to see, think, and feel. This step focuses on imagery. Our memories and imaginations have a sort of cinematic quality. We tend to remember events as if our eyes were the camera following the action. Having now poured out your initial take on your story to a friend, you can look back and ask yourself: what is the most important image in my story? In Tyler's story, mentioned at the start of this chapter, the most important image might be little Tyler, stuck in a muddy hole, being attacked by wasps. Whatever your most important image is, get it firmly in mind and go through the following steps:

1 Identify three salient emotions that are connected to that image.
2 Identify three salient words that are connect to that image.
3 Identify colors associated with the image.
4 Identify what sort of musical score might accompany the image in your mind.
5 Identify 1–3 people associated with that image.
6 Identify the central relationship associated with that image—perhaps a relationship between two people or between people and things.
7 Identify three words that describe that relationship.
8 Identify the change most associated with that image—what changes around it, what changes does it cause.

Again, it is useful to write the answers to these questions down in a notebook. Answering these questions will help you see the central image in your story with greater clarity. This will make the whole story easier to remember, and it will make it easier for you to make that image clear to your audience. When every image in your story is clear to you, you're not so much remembering a text as just describing what you see in your mind's eye.

Having identified and unpacked the central image of your story, it is now time to identify where that image lives in the structure of the story. Does it appear at the beginning? In the middle? At the end? Very often, the most important image of your story will be at the climax of the story—like the image of Tyler stuck in a muddy hole, surrounded by wasps. Right after that moment, Tyler's brother races in to save him. It exists right near the end of the story. Once you have a sense of where the most important image of your story rests, identify the most important images at other points in your story. In the case of Tyler's story, his most important image exists at the climax, so he would need to determine the beginning and very end of the story. Answer the questions above as they relate to the other images in your story. Once the central image is clear, you can build out either direction, identifying the images that precede and follow it. I like to think of these images like fence posts—poles that hold up the story and the narrative tissue that connects them.

With the central image of your story in mind, you can begin branching out and asking yourself other questions about other objects, settings, actions, and characters that occupy the story. The purpose here is to examine each of the elements, thus ensuring they are visible to you as a storyteller. Ask yourself the following questions:

1 What is the most important action in the story?
2 What is the most important object in the story?
3 What is the most important location or setting in the story?
4 What is one adjective that describes that location or setting?
5 What is the most important relationship in the story?
6 Who is the most important person in the story?
7 What is one adjective that describes that important person?
8 What is the most important image in the story?
9 What is the most important emotion in the story?
10 What is one adjective that describes the story?

As you are organizing and cataloging the images that represent the various parts of your story, it is worthwhile to consider the meaning or metaphor that those images contain. I've coached more than one story that begins with an airplane taking off—symbolizing a new journey ahead. The dark woods in Matt's story in Chapter 3 could be understood as symbolizing uncertainty. Storm clouds can stand for looming destruction or disorder. A sunrise can represent a new beginning, while a sunset can represent the closing of a particular chapter. You get the picture. The important thing is to consider the symbolic content of the images you've chosen and consider how you can maximize their impact on your story.

Step 3: Story Mapping

Mapping your story refers to any visual and/or tactile representation of the order of events. You're welcome to create any means of representing your story that makes sense to you, but it is useful to see the trajectory of your story as a physical shape. Most story maps track the progress or path of the protagonist of the story. In what follows, I offer a few different methods of mapping your story.

First, it can be a fun exercise to imagine what the path of your story would be like if it were a board game like *Candyland* or *Chutes & Ladders*. Both of these children's games feature a winding path that the player follows when they toss dice or draw game cards. In this exercise, imagine the protagonist of your story as the game piece, and each event as a new step on their path toward the ending. You can draw images that represent each step along the way and physically represent ups and downs, twists, and turns, with the shape of the pathway. You don't need to be a confident illustrator to create a basic game-inspired pathway that helps you think through the trajectory of your protagonist.

Second, grab note paper with sticky backing. On each piece of paper, write one important step along the way of your story—don't worry about writing them in order, just make sure you hit all the important bases. Spread these sticky notes out on a table and begin arranging them in order. Play around with the order of events by moving the sticky notes around. Once you've found an order that you like, find a large wall where you can place the sticky notes. Working from left to right, place the sticky notes on the wall in order. Consider the peaks and valleys of the story—where things get better and worse—and place the peaks and valleys at higher and lower places on the wall. When you step back, you'll have a visual representation or map of your story to help you visualize how the story moves through space.

Third, you can take some advice from author Kurt Vonnegut and his lesson about story shapes. You can find videos of Vonnegut—an accomplished and funny author whose work you may have encountered—describing his theories about story shapes, but I will summarize them here. In short, this is an exercise in graphing the shape of a story. He suggests beginning with a vertical axis, with "good fortune" at the top and "ill fortune" at the bottom. Next, he places a horizontal axis directly in the middle of the vertical axis, with "beginning" on the left end of the horizontal axis and "ending" on the right end of the horizontal axis. This middle point in the vertical axis represents circumstances that are normal or neither wonderful nor terrible. Anything above the line represents a positive change in fortune, and anything below the line represents a negative change in fortune. You begin mapping the trajectory by determining where your protagonist begins—either above the horizontal axis or below—depending on whether the story starts with things going well or going badly. Then you map the peaks and valleys of the story as the fortune of the protagonist changes.

This exercise allows you to see the rising and falling action of your story as the stakes increase and the fortunes of the protagonist change. It is important to remember that changes in fortune are relative to the circumstances in the story, not to the conditions of so-called "real life." For example, imagine you're telling a story about asking someone to the big dance in your early teenage days and subsequently being turned down. If you see these events now, with the benefit of hindsight, they might not seem all that important. Thus, the dip into ill fortune below the middle line would not be that big. However, if you put yourself back in your teenage shoes, these events may have felt very dramatic and important. From your point of view as a young person, the rejection may have resulted in a big dip into the ill fortune side of the graph.

Whichever mapping exercise you choose, pay close attention to the shape of the path that your story takes. If the trajectory of your story feels, for lack of a better word, "flat," you may need to either raise the stakes in your story or reconsider your choice in subject matter. Raising the stakes of your story means amplifying the peaks and valleys. It means clarifying to yourself and the audience why what you're talking about matters.

Mercy created a lovely story that was, on its face, about her church's food pantry winding up with far too many cartons of strawberries. She helped unload them and offered to deliver them to people who needed them, but still had a lot of strawberries left over. On its own, this is not a very dramatic story. However, when these events took place, Mercy was nearing graduation with an uncertain future, negotiating her first significant romantic relationship, and trying hard to meet the high personal and academic expectations she set for herself. When Mercy offered that context in the story, the strawberries took a metaphorical significance; an overwhelming (and unexpected) number of strawberries now stood in for the overwhelming and uncertain feelings she felt in that period of life. This shifted the stakes and significance of her story away from figuring out what to do with the strawberries, which offers low stakes, to figuring out what to do with her life, which felt more important. Adding this context amplified the peaks and valleys, the dramatic shape, of the map of her story.

Step 4: The Six Big Beats

When I began teaching storytelling years ago, I had no formal procedures in place. I asked an experienced colleague, who suggested I have students draw storyboards to compose their stories. I dutifully created dozens of storyboard handouts—six squares spread horizontally across a piece of paper, three on top and three on the bottom. I tried this method for a while, and, admittedly, it has its merits. However, I found that far too many of my students were uncomfortable with their skills as illustrators to allow this method to work. For many people, adding drawing to what was already an anxiety producing process only made things worse. So, I had all of these handouts with six storyboard boxes on them and no way to use them. I stuck them in a drawer. Eventually, as students began coming to my office to talk about their stories, I pulled out these sheets and began writing on them as scratch paper. I asked the students to tell me their story spontaneously (see step one), and I would write down key words in the six squares, rather than draw pictures, to help myself understand what they were driving at. To my surprise, I found that most (if not all) of my students' 7-to-10-minute stories could be easily broken down into 5 or 6 chapters or beats. More beats meant the story was too long and, in most cases, included a lot of superfluous material or unnecessary digressions. Fewer beats, like 3 or 4, usually meant the story was too short and needed to be expanded. Quite by accident, I discovered a simple means of breaking these narratives into digestible chunks.

You can easily make your own Big Beats worksheet by turning a piece of paper to the horizontal axis and drawing six boxes, three on the top and three on the bottom. I consider the box in the top left-hand corner to be Box 1 and the box on the bottom right-hand side to be Box 6. I suggest you begin with the last box: write the key words you need to capture the ending of your story. With that complete, go back to Box 1 and write in key words that you need to capture the beginning of the story. Once you've done that, find whatever you consider the middle (probably Box 4) and insert the key words you need to tell the climax or middle. From there, go back and fill in the remaining boxes with the information you need to get from the beginning to the middle and on to the end. Again, to be clear, only use key words in these boxes, so you're not too tempted to start composing a piece of literature.

Set your Big Beats in front of you and keep them out of your hands as you start telling your story. Use the Big Beats as notes but don't become too attached to them. Allow the performance to develop organically as you speak it. Stay on your feet and tell the story numerous times. As you get more and more comfortable with it, you can continue to add descriptive language and vivid imagery. You can play around with the order of events. For instance, it is often useful to swap Boxes 1 and 2 because many people begin in Box 1 with exposition and the action doesn't start until they arrive at Box 2 (remember our discussion of beginning in media res?). You can work out transitions that keep you moving from one idea to another. The more you say it out loud, the more solid and strong the story should become. As you repeat the story over and over again, it should become ingrained in your body, so you don't just remember it—you truly learn it.

Step 5: Rehearsal and Memory

Repeating the story over and over again should help it take shape, but you still have to remember the words you want to say in your story, even if it is not formally scripted. In what follows, we'll talk about some ways to improve your ability to remember your story.

Visualization is your first line of defense against the danger of forgetting the words you want to say. I suggest you associate visual imagery that you can see clearly in your mind's eye with every one of the Big Beats of your story. If you can see the scene or events of your story, you can simply describe what you see rather than try to memorize specific language. Furthermore, if you need to include highly specific language, you can associate the image in your mind's eye with that language so that when you "see" the scene, you'll remember the words you want to say. It is a bit like creating a movie in your mind that you can describe to the audience. I tell a story about the dramatic events that surrounded my daughter's birth. I vividly remember the nurses rushing my wife into surgery for an emergency cesarean delivery, and I clearly remember them bringing me the baby to hold while they took care of my wife. When I tell that story, I barely have to think about the words I want to say because I can simply remember the imagery and report what I "see" to the audience.

Next, connecting specific language to specific vocal, physical, and performative choices will help you remember what you want to say. For many people, associating a particular piece of text with a particular physical gesture helps them remember what to say. You may remember Courtney's story about the goat on the roof from Chapter 3. This was the first story she had told, and Courtney struggled to remember the order of events in her story. In the rehearsal process, we added physicality along with most of the language. Right after the very first line ("The goat is on the roof") she says, "Ever since I could conceive of the idea of 'dog' I knew that's what I wanted in my life." When she says "conceive" she holds her hand up and out, as if there is a small idea resting in her hand. When she says "dog" she accompanies the word with a gesture: both hands raised together and then spread apart, as if she was framing the words on a marquee above a theater. When she says "that's what I wanted in my life" she gives the audience a pointed index finger to punctuate "that's". She did this combination of language and gesture throughout the story, and it helped Courtney remember the story.

In just the same way you can connect particular moments in your story to physicality and gesture, you can also connect that language to sounds that are memorable. The spoken word has all the qualities of music, and those musical qualities can charge words with meaning. The word *prosody* is a catch-all term for the stress, rhythm, and intonation in spoken language. The use of prosody not only makes your story sound more musical, but it can also help you remember your story. For example, you can imagine using a causal, even monotone voice to say the phrase, "itty, bitty, teeny, tiny." But, when I squeeze the sound of my voice, close the spaces between the words, and say it quickly, the phrase might sound like, "ittybittyteenytiny." The phrase sounds compressed and smaller, reflecting the meaning of the phrase itself. What's more, it makes the part of the story easier to remember because it is no longer a simple piece of text; it is an action and a sound.

Perhaps the best way to ensure that you can remember your story is to include lots of things that you enjoy saying and doing. Create moments that stand out to you: dramatic pauses, twists and turns, jokes, vivid images—anything that you like describing or enjoy saying. I imagine these moments like bright bulbs on a string of decorative lights. The story connects these bright moments, but the bulbs make it easy to see how you can get from one bright spot to the next. For example, in Ben's story about the death of his friend (described in Chapter 4), he tells a series of "chemistry jokes" that he and his nerdy pals would tell while hiking on Boy Scout trips. "I would tell you a few chemistry jokes," he tells the audience, "but all the good chemistry jokes argon." He then goes on to tell a litany of these jokes—jokes designed to make the audience groan and delight at how corny they are. Ben would never, ever forget this section of the story because it evoked a strong visual image in his mind, it was connected the physicality of his delivery, it incorporated the vocal prosody of the set up and punchline, and most of all: he loved telling those jokes. The bright spot those jokes represented illuminated the way to the next part of the story he loved to tell, making it easy to remember the entire story.

When it comes to rehearsing your story, there are no shortcuts and very few tricks. You must put in the work to ensure that you have it down cold before you perform it for an audience. That being said, over the years, I have noticed a few useful approaches to rehearsal. First, as I mentioned when describing how to you use the Six Big Beats, you need to stand up on your feet during your initial rehearsal process. Standing up makes your body engaged and alert. Stand up and tell your story, and once you reach the end, start over again immediately without stopping to fret, get a drink of water, or take a break. Keep that pattern going—repeating the story on your feet without stopping—four or five times. You will probably find that after the fifth time repeating the story without stopping, two things will happen. First, you'll probably have a relatively strong command of the material, and second, you'll find a new level of emotional depth in the performance. Rehearsing your story repeatedly without stopping can be a little taxing on your body. It can wear you out. That can make you vulnerable and being vulnerable, makes you sound and appear more authentic.

Once you've got that material well in hand, it can be useful to rehearse in a setting where you're already doing something else. Rehearsing while you're driving, taking a shower, putting dishes away in the cupboard—any rote behavior that doesn't take much attention but distracts you enough that you don't focus on yourself and become self-conscious. This approach allows you to get the story into your body while also getting other important daily tasks done.

Finally, whenever you rehearse your story, it is useful to visualize yourself performing the story successfully. This may sound a little corny, but positive visualization helps you imagine success. Athletes, businesspeople, and artists all utilize this technique to prime themselves for success. In your case, imagine yourself in the place you plan to perform. Imagine yourself calm and comfortable. Imagine everyone in the audience responding just as you'd like them to respond. Picture it until it is vivid in your mind's eye. Hold on to those images. It may sound silly, but I strongly believe that visualizing success is important for manifesting that success in the real world.

In this chapter, we've looked at some ways of composing your story before you ever need to engage in writing in the traditional sense. As I think back to Tyler, whose story appears at the end of this chapter, I believe that working from action to text made it possible for him to step over the roadblocks that can get in the way of good storytelling and arrive at a heartwarming destination. With your story mapped out, in the next chapter we'll begin discussing how you can use language and figures of speech to maximum effect.

Questions to Consider

1 Have you had experiences that made writing seem daunting? When did they happen? Why do you think they happened? How can you reimagine those experiences in a positive way?
2 Where are the good rehearsal spaces in your life? Do you have a room of your own? Can you reserve a room in a public library? Do you have a commute that gives you time alone in the car? Think about the rehearsal spaces available to you.

"Super Jeff"
Created and Performed by Tyler Thompson

Okay. Okay. Okay. So, I was five years old and I was hanging out with my big brother, Jeff. And when you're five years old and you're hanging out with my big brother Jeff, it's less about wanting to be like Jeff and much more about wanting Jeff to like you and think you're cool. And my big brother Jeff was cool. I mean, he was way taller than me, he had way more friends than me, and he had that badass collection of Jurassic Park action figures. It was dope.

On this particular day, we were hanging out with Jeff's best friend, Joey. How do I describe Joey? Joey, he was an only child. He watched his language. He rode a bike with a helmet. Joey owned cats.

Now, the plan for today was that we were going to go to the back behind Joey's house to this old, big, empty, muddy creek bed and build a bridge, which was awesome because none of us knew how to build a bridge, so we're just going to build one.

First half hour went great. We created these cross-section hatches that interlocked at intersecting intervals to support the bridge's focal point of structure. Mostly, what we were doing was digging holes in the mud and putting sticks in the holes.

And everything was going fine until suddenly, out of nowhere, Joey slaps his neck. *[Slaps neck]* And we all start to see these little black dots moving around in the air. And we notice that we're surrounded by these things. And that's when Joey yells, *[Shouting]* "Mud daubers!"

Mud daubers are these tiny little wasps that live in mud, and essentially, when you try to build bridges, they come out and they kill everybody. So Joey, being the kind of kid who watches his language, yells, "Darn it!" out of the creek, hightails it back to his house. My brother Jeff follows suit, jumps out of the creek, hightails it back to Joey's house. I try to follow suit, but I can't because I'm five and I'm surrounded by wasps.

But man, I'm trying, and I'm digging out of that hole *[motions digging]* and I'm sliding deeper and deeper down, and the hole's getting muddier and bigger and wider, and I'm surrounded by these mud daubers, and while this is going on, two things are happening in my brain simultaneously. Firstly, "I'm going to die here." And secondly, but most importantly, "This is not cool. I'm not impressing anyone. It's very embarrassing. If my big brother Jeff were here, he'd… Wait a minute, my big brother Jeff left me here."

And that's when I hear it. "Donk, donk, donk, donk, donk." It's Jeff running back through the woods. He came back for me. Jeff leaps into the creek, literally grabs me by the shirt, hurls me out, leaps out behind me, grabs me by the arm, and we both run back to Joey's, toward salvation.

Okay. I got stung once, right here. [*Points to stomach*] Still hurts. Jeff and Joey got obliterated. I mean, Jeff's face looked like a Star Wars alien, which we always thought would be really cool, just not under these circumstances. And they were fine in the end, the swelling went down, but it was a harried experience.

Basically, I tell this story for two reasons. Firstly, it's the beginning of my war against all insect life on the planet. And second thing, but most importantly, it's the end of wanting Jeff to like me and the beginning of wanting to be like Jeff. He's my role model. He's always there for me. I can count on him. Jeff is my hero.

6 "If Math Class Were Here, I Would Fight Math Class": Using Language and Figures of Speech

Kit had a bottomless well of stories about outlaw adventures that happened in their youth. Some people just don't fit neatly into the boxes dominant culture sets out for us, and Kit was definitely one of those people. That—and an affection for outlaw behavior in general— were probably the reasons why they were asked to leave public school and were enrolled in a private high school. As Kit tells it, they felt like private school was like prison, and they needed to be the toughest new kid on the block. The pressure in the private school continued to build until one day, while sitting in math class, they had a panic attack and launched an ill-fated escape attempt that ended with Kit in the freezing cold Chattahoochee River. That day in math class, it seemed, was the final straw. "I hated math class," Kit said in the story. "If math class were here right now, I would fight math class." The strategy of addressing "math class" as if it were a person is called *apostrophe*. While the events of the story were dramatic and a little traumatic, Kit wanted the story to have a lighthearted tone. Kit swapped a painful description of the pressure of the private school for a very clever line that turned math class into their anthropomorphic nemesis. Kit's story had a lot of great moments, but this small choice of words lit up what might otherwise have been an unremarkable spot in the story.

I love language and have loved it for as long as I can remember. I love rhymes, I love the sound of words, I love learning word origins, and I love a good turn of phrase. I love poetry and pop songs—both brimming with evocative imagery and charged with emotion. More than anything, I love language that lives in performance. Growing up on a farm in Nebraska, I learned plenty of colorful (and sometimes profane) sayings to describe the trials and joys of everyday life. Odds are good that you too can remember rhymes you learned as a child, songs you learned at summer camp, and dirty jokes you learned on the school bus—all because the language, when performed, is meaningful and memorable.

In this chapter, we'll discuss figures of speech, language, and wit and the ways they can be deployed for maximum effect. I do not offer an exhaustive review of figures of speech (for reasons that will become clear) but, rather, discuss how a handful of common figures of speech function. This

DOI: 10.4324/9781003039266-6

should get your mental wheels turning so that you can start creating your own impressive and evocative language. Becoming proficient in the use of figures of speech, language, and wit can take a lifetime, and it is, in a very real sense, a process that never ends. To me, that is part of the pleasure of using language—there is always another eloquent turn of phrase waiting for you around the corner.

What Are Figures of Speech?

Simply put, a figure of speech is the non-literal use of words or phrases to evoke meaning. We use figures of speech to bring forth an intended image or to charge a moment with a desired meaning. However, I do not mean to imply that figures of speech only serve a rhetorical purpose—to simply communicate an idea. They do that, but figures of speech also serve an aesthetic purpose right alongside their rhetorical purpose. Hyperbole, metaphor, personification, and so on can decorate our speech. Just as you might wear a costume for a play or wear your best clothes for a special event, figures of speech dress up your language to make it special for public consumption. Figures of speech can also be imagined, like the architecture of your story. It holds the story up, supports it, and gives it character. In what follows, we'll look at some simple and useful figures of speech.

This is, by no means, an exhaustive list of figures of speech, but it will start you on your way toward your own imaginative use of language. I encourage you to remember this: there is no quiz at the end of this chapter, and bright-line distinctions between these categories are not particularly important (at least not to me). The proof that you understand language exists in your ability to use it, not in your ability to define all the terms. To paraphrase author E.B. White, explaining a figure of speech is like dissecting a frog. You understand it better, but the frog dies in the process. With that vivid and gruesome comparison in mind, let's slice up some frogs.

Hyperbole

Simply put, hyperbole is exaggeration or overstatement. This exaggeration is deployed to capture how something feels or what it means in a nonliteral sense. Sometimes, when I have a cold, my nose is the size of a Buick. Once, I waited in line so long to renew my driver's license, I had to go home and shave before they took my picture. Given the opportunity, I would eat a metric ton of nachos. Obviously, none of these statements are true. But they capture the essence of a feeling. It should also be clear by now that hyperbole is most often used for comic effect. The comic effect and evocative power of hyperbole are enhanced by specificity: it's not just a car, it's a Buick; the wait is so long I grew a beard; it's not just a ton of nachos, it's a metric ton. When used for comic effect, hyperbole fulfills two roles: illustrating a feeling and making your story more entertaining.

Understatement

One could argue that understatement if the opposite of hyperbole—downplaying something to highlight how big or important it actually is. Understatement is often dependent on sarcasm, which is the subtle art of saying the opposite of what you mean. "As soon as I backed my car completely through the garage door, I knew I was in a little bit of trouble," is the kind of understatement I imagine ringing out loud and clear. By stating that "I knew I was in a little bit of trouble," in what is a pretty serious situation, the listener is pointed back to just how serious the situation is. Sometime after Kit (the storyteller at the start of this chapter) was sent to private school, they were shipped off to a wilderness camp for delinquent youth. The group of young women at the camp became determined to catch, cook, and eat a wild turkey. After much struggle, they caught their turkey, only to have the counselors point out that this was a national park and killing the turkey would be a federal crime. Kit's eyes go wide, and they deadpan, "This was news." The understatement got a big laugh and underscored just how little they'd thought this plan through.

Kidding on the Square

Somewhere in between hyperbole and understatement is a fun rhetorical device known as kidding on the square. In old-fashioned slang, "on the square" or "being square" with someone meant being honest with them. Kidding on the square incorporates humor without undercutting the honesty of the statement. For example, your friend might say to you, "Yeesh, the color of that sweater is ugly—just kidding!" and in that context, you'd suppose they don't mean that your sweater is ugly but, instead, they're simply teasing you. However, if your friend said, "the color of that sweater makes it look like a yak puked on you,"—you might discern that they are joking, but they honestly don't like your sweater. As I mentioned before, one student started a story about getting along with his many siblings by gesturing to himself, giving an exasperated look, and saying this line: "It's hard … being the smartest person in your family." The line got a big laugh, and it set up his cynicism which, over the course of the story, gets softened by his family's love. But catch him after the show and ask him if he really thinks he's the smartest person in his family, and he'll tell that is, in fact, the case. He's joking, but he means it. He's kidding on the square.

Metaphor

Most of you probably already know that metaphor is, at its core, the comparison of two things. Often, metaphors compare one thing that is abstract and/or unknown to something that is concrete and/or known to the reader or listener. If I were to tell you, "My friend Nick is dumber than a box of hammers," you might first think, "Wow, he's not very nice to his friend Nick." But once you got over that, you might understand that Nick isn't very smart.

While the sentiment is a little mean, there is something lovely about the way the weight and density of a hammer communicate my imaginary friend's stupidity. The comparison invites the listener to instantly consider the flexibility, agility, and buoyancy that we often associate with intelligence contrasted with the density and rigidity of a hammer. My imaginary friend isn't just a little bit dense; he's as dense, heavy, and inflexible as a whole box of hammers. When describing a car crash in a story, Laura exclaimed, "the front of my boyfriend's car folded over like a warm tortilla … of pain." Not only did this comparison make the experience clear, but her reference to a tortilla was also her way of pointing at her Puerto Rican heritage, that popped up throughout the story. Just like hyperbole, metaphor works best when it is specific, and just like hyperbole, metaphor helps to capture a feeling rather than report a fact.

Anaphora

This simple figure of speech repeats the same word or phrase at the beginning of successive clauses or sentences. One of the most famous instances of this figure of speech is attributed to Julius Caesar who is said to have declared—*Veni, vidi, vici*—which translates to, "I came, I saw, I conquered." In this case, the absence of conjunctions between the clauses drives home the quick and decisive nature of Caesar's victory. You could just as easily imagine a story about the breakup with a line like, "she walked in, she handed me my ring, she turned around a left." In this example, the speed and decisiveness end the relationship. Or you could imagine a story about planning a party with a line like, "You don't need food to have a party, you don't need drinks to have a party, and you don't need money to have a party—you just need a plan." In this case, the anaphora drives home that you don't need much to have a good time. Like many figures of speech, anaphora draws attention to a particular idea by decorating it with heightened language.

Personification

Personification is the attribution of human characteristics to non-human things. The classic animal fables you may have heard as a child offer obvious examples of personification. However, you can imagine any number of interesting ways to use personification in personal narrative storytelling. Imagine, for example, that your roommate left pizza in the refrigerator and told you not to eat it. Instead of saying, "I really wanted that pizza," you might say, "the pizza began calling to me, beckoning me to take a bite." Or imagine you're telling a story about your car breaking down. You might begin by saying, "I went out that morning, tried to start my car, but the engine had clearly decided to take the day off." Pizza can't seduce you, and engines can't take a personal day—people do those things. But the use of personification draws you and the audience into a more meaningful relationship with the non-human things in your story.

Apostrophe

In the beginning of this chapter, I noted that Kit's decision to address math class as if it were a person is an example of an apostrophe. I like to think of this as a reverse camera angle on personification. Instead of giving an inanimate object human qualities so that it can act on you, the apostrophe allows you to act on the inanimate object as if it were human. As you can see from the math class example, this can be an effective and fun figure of speech to deploy.

Chiasmus

For reasons that are not clear to me, I have a special place in my heart for chiasmus. This figure of speech repeats words, concepts, or grammatical structures in reverse order. President John F. Kennedy famously used chiasmus in the line, "Ask not what your country can do for you, ask what you can do for your country" and when he quipped, "Never let us negotiate out of fear, but let us never fear to negotiate." Dr. Mardy Grothe compiled a whole book on the subject of chiasmus, called *Never Let a Fool Kiss You or a Kiss Fool You*. I once heard someone spin this impressive play on words: "you catch more flies with honey, but you catch more honeys when you're fly." These figures of speech make an idea dynamic and memorable in the ears of a listener.

Ideogram

An ideogram is any word in a short phrase that expresses a powerful ideological concept. For example, words with positive associations like "freedom," or "rights" and words with negative associations such as "liar" or "terrorist" all point to a much larger history of ideas behind these simple words. These terms are always highly situated in a particular time, place, and set of cultural conditions. What seems positive in one context may be negative in another. Ideographs are often used in political discourse and advertising to evoke an emotional response from the listener, by associating a product or an idea with these kinds of emotionally charged terms. If, for instance, a political candidate calls their opponent "soft on crime," they are not only questioning their policies; they are also associating their opponent with softness or weakness—two qualities not typically valued by many voters. In storytelling, one can deploy ideograms to point the audience in a particular ideological direction.

The Infinite Possibilities of Language

This is just a short list of a few common figures of speech that we have found useful over the years. Our goal here has not been to offer an exhaustive list of figures of speech. Instead, I want to get you thinking about the ways you can use language to capture the precise meaning, tone, and sensibility that you're searching for. While language has boundaries and words have meanings that we all agree upon, the possible combinations of words to create meaning are practically infinite. That might feel overwhelming at times, but I encourage you to think of it like a game. Rolling an idea around in your head and trying to find the best way to say it can be rewarding. Trying lines out loud to yourself can make you laugh all by itself. Kicking phrases back and forth between friends until you land on just the right one can simply be a great time.

As of this writing, I am working with a student on a story that is about, among other things, his trans identity. The subject is delicate because here in the United States transgender people face violence and discrimination in employment, healthcare, encounters with law enforcement and on and on. Part of his purpose is to speak frankly with the audience to help people understand and normalize his identity. We're still working on the story, but early on he has a line that goes something like this: "I'm trans. If you don't know, that means that when I came out of my mother's womb the doctor said, 'It's a girl!'" but when I came out to my parents 18 years later, I said, 'It's a boy!'" Every time I hear this line, it lights me up inside. I find it so crisp and clever. One of the best parts of working on stories with my students is that it allows them to be precisely who they want to be and get a whole room full of people to come along for the ride. Language is a crucial tool in that process. I believe that line, with its parallel structure and cheeky twist, defuses the tension this topic can produce while simultaneously putting the storyteller firmly in the driver's seat. That he is able to so deftly articulate this complex topic in simple terms implicitly tells the audience they are in safe hands. I also have a feeling that using clever language to describe his identity can productively intervene in the sour attitudes of folks who harbor harmful anti-trans attitudes.

This chapter was all about language. In what follows, you can read Kit's story mentioned earlier. The title 'With Regards to Alan Jackson" refers to the country singer and his famous song about the Chattahoochee River, which plays a crucial role in the story. I hope you can see the way Kit uses language to paint a vivid picture of these events. Chapter 7 focuses on embodiment or physicalizing your storytelling performance. Language and embodiment, go hand-in-hand because how you say something is just as important as what you say. But for now, I hope your brain is churning, considering all the possibilities that language can hold for you.

Questions to Consider

1 Which figure of speech in this chapter is your favorite? Make a list of as many examples of that figure of speech as you can.
2 Go back to the stories you've read in previous chapters. Where can you find figures of speech being used in those other stories?
3 What is the most vivid way that you can describe the central event in your story? Try describing it to a friend with the best evocative language you can muster.

With Regards to Alan Jackson
Created and Performed by Kit Fay

It's hard to tell looking at me now, but I was sort of a weird kid. 16 is, I think, kind of universally bizarre because you haven't been a person long enough to really know what you're doing, but you have been one exactly long enough to think you know [*points at audience*]. Missteps are inevitable. I missed a couple staircases, and by the time I was 16, I didn't have much going for me other than a promising future as a drug dealer. [*Puts hands on hips*] I ended up in boarding school.

Now I imagined boarding school sort of the same way I imagined prison. I was going to go in there. I was going to find the toughest kid, and I was going to crush them. From then on, it would be smooth sailing. So I walked through the hall on my first day of school in my short plaid skirt and my knee-high navy socks, practicing my snarl. [*Snarls*] It didn't take me long, however, to realize that, I don't know if you guys know this, boarding school is not like prison.

These kids were nice, respectable, and clean [*makes a grossed-out face*], and exactly the opposite of all of my friends. I knew that they wouldn't like me, so I decided to hate them first as a precaution [*hands on hip*]. I spent the next couple of weeks sending mean texts under the table [*texts on an imaginary phone*] and making mean faces and smoking cigarettes [*pretending to smoke a cigarette*] by myself behind the auditorium. I was the baddest bitch in school. Until one day, sitting in math class. Now, I hate math class. I would fight math class right now. Anyways.

It was never a good day when I was in math class, and today I was having more trouble than usual following the lecture. [*Begins to squirm and scratch*] My skin started crawling, the walls started closing in, and my lungs shrank to the size of peanuts. And this was not my first rodeo. I knew what a panic attack felt like. I also knew that having a panic attack in math class would do nothing for my bad bitch persona. So I raised my hand [*raises hand*] and I asked to be excused.

And I calmly got up, walked out the door, down the hall, passed the bathrooms, out of the building, and into the sunlight [*with arms outstretched*]. When I stepped outside, everything got very still, and the buzzing in my head stopped and I could breathe again. And it was at this point that I started thinking, well, Kit, if you turn around and go back now, it'll be like nothing happened. I continued to think this as I walked away from the building and towards the hill that would lead me off school property.

I didn't have a plan. I was just moving along. There was a guard tower station, not a tower, but a station. So I decided I was going to climb over the fence and into someone's backyard. So I do this in my skirt, and I hear a dog snarling and a man yelling. This seems like too much to deal with, so I climb back over the fence and decide to take my chances with the guard. As I near the station, it appears, to my luck, that it is empty.

Unluckily, as I am leaving school property [*motions running*], the guard himself pulls up in his white van. He leans out the window (appears to be leaning out a window), and he looks at me and he says, "What are you doing? You can't leave." To which I said, [*mouth open makes no noise*], and kept moving. At some point, I hear him say something into a walkie-talkie, and that is the last thing I heard because I was off running. I took off through a series of yards, through a side yard, and then I'm in people's backyard, climbing over fences, jumping off of things, falling, and getting up.

Not even noticing because fear and adrenaline are like a super-power. I keep running until I get to the bank of one of the widest parts of the Chattahoochee River. The water is moving really fast here. I haven't mentioned until this point that it's February, but it's about to be really relevant. Despite all the planning and foresight that I've given to every decision I've made in my life thus far; I close my eyes. [*Closes eyes*] I take a deep breath, and I jump [*arms out like to jump*] into the Chattahoochee River.

I crash to the bottom [*stomps*], and then I bob up in the cold water, and it's real cold [*makes swimming motions*]. What am I doing? I realize that the far bank of the river is a sheer rock face. But never fear; there's a ladder straight across the river. Now, I didn't think this through, but turns out one does not swim [*doggie paddle motions*] straight across the river as it is [*makes motion to imply moving*]. I realize pretty quickly that my options are to hope that the far shore levels out before I pull a Rasputin and die of hypothermia, turn around, and swim back to the shore.

So I turn around, I pull myself up in the mud, and I sit there and I wait for someone to find me. And find me they did. I was escorted back into school [*arms look restrained*] by all of the administrators, the guard, and both of my parents. I have long since lost my shoes. My little plaid skirt and my knee-high socks are covered in mud. Everyone is watching. I would love to tell you that this was the last in my series of teenage misadventures, but shit happens. I still had a lot of steps to miss. I can tell you, however, that people stopped thinking of me as the snarly weird girl who didn't talk to anyone and started thinking of me as the snarly weird badass who said, fuck math class and jumped in a river.

7 "I Think About the Mask on My Face and I Wonder How Long It'd Been Since I Put It on": Communicating Meaning Through Embodied Performance

Mace was talking about the body. Not just any body, but their body and what it meant to them and to the people around them. Mace's story, which we called "Housewarming," follows them as they prepare to attend what they refer to as their first "gay housewarming party." It was a costume party, so they put on a mask and got dressed up, a little uncertain what the evening would hold. Upon arriving at the extravagant costume affair, Mace's old friend warmly welcomed them and asked, "so, what are you?" Mace knew that they were not "straight" or "cis and straight" but, at the time, they were not yet sure exactly what that meant for them. This question from a friend pulls Mace, the storyteller, down a rabbit hole of memories detailing uncertainty, insecurity, and mean-spirited teasing from peers. Mace always knew they were different, but they were never sure how. When Mace sheepishly admitted, "I don't know" their old friend enthusiastically replied, "Isn't it marvelous?"

I was taken with Mace's story the first time I heard it. When we returned to campus after the advent of a global pandemic, I was looking for ways to tell stories that were not face-to-face. I settled on having students in one of my introductory classes write and record stories in an audio format. I loved (and still do) the way Mace described the experience of ambiguity about gender and sexuality and the way that ambiguity affects one's sense of place in the world. When Mace joined my advanced storytelling course, I suggested they remount their original story, this time for our outdoor socially distanced spring showcase. In one sense, the story was done. Mace had already written and recorded it. But writing, reading, and recording a story is one thing. Performing it live in front of an audience is something else altogether. Transitioning from a recorded medium to a live performance introduced Mace's performing body into the equation. Bringing the performers' body into the story felt right because so much of Mace's story is about the body: about what the body feels, what we call those feelings, what the body desires, how the body recognizes itself, and how Mace's body is read by people in the world. The "mask" mentioned in the title of this chapter refers to Mace's literal mask worn to the costume party and, simultaneously, the metaphorical mask they'd been wearing to hide their emerging true self. It is a neat trick of language to

DOI: 10.4324/9781003039266-7

play on the double meaning of the mask. The use of mask-as-metaphor usually implies the existence of some truer, more authentic self, hidden below the surface. When Mace put their story on stage, it came to life. Their timing enhanced the humor and drama of the story. Their gestures and voices brought the other people in the story to life. The tension Mace wound up and released from their body physicalized the arch of anxiety and catharsis present in the story. I like to think that their "true self" was more fully embodied when Mace put their story live on stage.

In this chapter, we're going to look at embodiment in storytelling from multiple points of view. We'll define just what we mean by "embodiment," describe some aspects of embodiment, explore the performance of characters in your story, and finally examine timing, pause, and the power of silence and stillness. Throughout this chapter, I encourage you to put this book down and begin putting these concepts into your body and speaking them out loud. After all, storytelling is an embodied practice; you can only make a story come alive through action.

What Do We Mean by "Embodiment"?

Embodiment in performance is a kind of deliberate nonverbal communication. Broadly speaking, this communication has affective and practical purposes. These two functions do not exist discretely, but it is useful to discuss them one at a time. First, the affective dimension of embodiment refers to the expression of feelings, attitudes, and moods. In this way, embodiment makes otherwise abstract concepts or feelings into something that can be seen by an audience. Imagine someone laughing and jumping. We might describe this as an embodiment of happiness. Alternatively, imagine someone weeping with their head in their hands. This might be an embodiment of sadness. The laughing and weeping are not the happiness and sadness. Happiness and sadness are feelings. The laughing and weeping are outwardly directed, visible, and embodiment of those feelings. These are simple examples, but imagine more complex feelings like insecurity, anxiety, or denial. How would you communicate these abstract concepts through your body without using words? If, as I suggested at the start of this book, storytelling is about getting a group of people to see, think, and feel the same thing at the same time, then embodiment is the way we make those abstract intangible feelings come to life for the audience.

Embodiment can also be more practical than the expression of affect. For example, gestures can be used in performance to underscore language. Imagine you're telling a story and you say, "there was no way I was ever telling my mother about this." When you say, "no way" you might fan your fingers out in front of you, cross your hands, and wave them apart—a very common gesture that means "no." Or, when describing a long trip, you might cross your arm across your body, extend your index finger, and then let that finger travel a wide arch in the other direction to underscore the long distance you traveled. When describing two different choices—living at home with your parents or moving to an apartment with a friend—you might gesture out with your left hand as you describe the first choice and gesture out with your right hand as you describe the second choice, leaving both hands in front of you and divided to demonstrate the separate space these two choices occupy.

Embodiment goes beyond the use of your hands to gesture. Posture is another way we use the body to create meaning. Think back to the example where you describe two choices—live at home or live with a friend—and use gestures to separate them. Now imagine that when you gesture and refer to living at home, your posture slumps, and when you gesture and refer to living with a friend, your posture straightens and leans eagerly forward. In this example, we've capitalized on the practical use of gestures and added an affective dimension expressed by your posture. Just think about how much meaning is communicated when someone rolls their eyes in disgust or lets out a deep, exasperated sigh. Facial expressions, the tilt of your head, the way you shuffle your feet, a deep breath in—these are all ways that we use the body to communicate meaning. It is far beyond the scope of this book to try and enumerate all the possible ways the body can express itself. Nor is there just one right way to express yourself through the body.

Kit, who appears elsewhere in this book, often included an awkward, nervous shrug in their stories that could get a reaction from an audience by itself. I wouldn't have thought to tell Kit to shrug nervously, but it worked. Kit's shrug feels like proof that who you are and what you do naturally is the best guidebook for deciding how to use your body to express yourself. It is, I think, fair to say that the body can't help but communicate meaning merely by its presence. That means you can't do it incorrectly. Whoever you are is good, and whoever you are is enough. However, it is your job to be aware of what your body is doing and to give some thought and rehearsal to putting your natural way of moving through the world to its fullest use. For instance, gestures that are shaky or too passive may make you look nervous. Gesturing a great deal will deaden the impact of any particular use of gesture you intend to be meaningful because it will be lost in the "noise," so to speak, of your erratic body. Alternatively, if you pause and are still for a moment, you can communicate a great deal by subtly pursing your lips because your lips will have everyone's attention. The question is not whether you are using your body correctly or incorrectly, but whether body is communicating what you would like it to communicate.

Representation and Presentation

Representation and presentation are two different styles of performance that suggest two different approaches to embodiment. For the most part, embodiment in storytelling has a representational quality. But sometimes, storytellers oscillate between these two approaches in one performance. Therefore, it is worthwhile to distinguish between representation and presentation in performance. If you have ever acted in a play, seen a play, or watched a film, you are already familiar with what I call a presentational style of performance. When a performer takes up a presentational style, they act in the moment as if the action is happening in real time. In plays, for example, actors usually have props. If their character is meant to pick up a cup and drink, the actor has a cup, picks up the cup, and drinks. If the actor's character is sad and crying, the actor will most likely do the work to shed some real tears. The actor is not shifting between the present and the past; they are firmly grounded in "now" and that "now" is meant to be understood as real.

A representational style of performance does just what the name implies—it represents, or suggests, the action rather than fully embodying it. Whereas a presentational style presents the character's affect as if it is happening in real time—in the here and now—a representational style more subtly indicates that the story is happening now *and* then, depending on the intention of the storyteller. By its very nature, personal narrative storytelling relates a story that happened in the past. However, often, storytellers tack back and forth between embodying the story as if they are experiencing it in the present while narrating the events of the past. If there is a part of your story that you'd like to emphasize, you might draw attention to it by shifting into a more presentational style in that moment.

For example, early in Mace's story, described at the start of this chapter, they describe trying to decide what to wear to the "gay housewarming party." They turn slightly to the side to pantomime going through clothes hanging in a closet, all the while talking in the past tense about the anxiety they felt about their evolving identity. Mace does not pantomime putting on the final outfit; they just describe what it was. They then turn to face an imaginary mirror and look at themselves before shifting into the next part of the story. This example illustrates the ways a storyteller can shift between presentational and representational styles in some moments. Storytellers are, in this way, shapeshifters who pass back and forth between "there-then" and "here-now" as it suits their purposes. Personally, I feel like this shapeshifting is a kind of storytelling superpower that has existed as far back as ancient people gathered around a fire, telling tales of the hunt.

How do you decide when to represent something physically and when to rely on narration? There are several ways to answer this question. As a rule, you can feel very comfortable physicalizing something that you are describing as happening in real time. On the other hand, you can usually skip that kind of physicalizing when you are stepping out of the action to describe how you felt about what is happening. Of course, as with all rules, this is not always true. Imagine, for example, you're telling a story about your dad insisting that you dig up a flower bed on a Saturday morning when you wanted to go out with your friends. You might subtly pantomime digging up the dirt while describing how frustrated you felt about missing out on fun with your friends. Imagine that, as your frustration grows, each thrust of the pantomimed shovel becomes more aggressive until the frustration peaks and you throw down the imaginary shovel. This example illustrates the way that narration and physicalizing action could come together to drive home your point. As with all things in storytelling, you need to ask yourself: what work does this choice do in the story I'm telling? If you can't answer this question to your own satisfaction, you may not be making the best choice.

Embodying Characters

Taking on the persona of the characters in your story can be one of the most enjoyable parts of performing your story. Little touches of physicality can bring the people who appear in your story to life, giving the story depth and texture that would otherwise be missing. As I explained earlier, most traditional acting is presentational—the actor fully embodies the character they are playing. Storytelling is mostly representational, so the performer might play multiple characters in one story, and those characters are suggested rather than fully embodied. The suggestion of a character allows the performer to deftly slip into the character, back out into the narrative, and back again as needed. The suggestion of a character, rather than full immersion in a character, means the character may feel somewhat one-dimensional. That is okay. Most of the time, characters in your story serve a purpose. We're not meant to understand them in the fullness of their identity; we're meant to understand the role they play in your particular tale.

There are several ways to suggest the presence of a character. Sometimes a shift in posture will communicate a shift in character. Sometimes a gesture can help define a character. Sometimes a change in your vocal quality can simply signal a character. Sometimes a combination of all three things will easily bring a character to life. For instance, Micah worked up a story about going to summer camp as a kid and getting scared when a counselor told them all about the legend of the pig man. Micah tells the pig man story in the first person as the counselor. He shifts his posture, turns to the side, and adopts a thick southern accent he felt was in keeping with the spirit of the counselors he had at camp. The effect is very funny, which is Micah's intention. It is also a fairly one-dimensional representation of the counselor, but the counselor serves a function in the story. They are not meant to be a fully realized character. Micah's subtle physical and vocal shifts help to bring the characters to life so they can serve their purpose in the story.

Pause, Stillness, and Timing

Although narrative is the focus of storytelling, one could argue that time is one of the primary mediums of storytelling. Or, to use a metaphor, we can think of narrative as paint, while time is both the canvas and the brush. Storytellers tell stories in which time passes, and time also passes in real time as the story is told. That means manipulating time through the use of embodied performance, is central to storytelling. Storytellers primarily manipulate time through the rate at which the speak and move and through the strategic use of pause and timing.

Storytellers can easily manipulate the audience's sense of time in the story through performance. If, for example, you are talking about all the errands you had to run on a particular morning, you might deliver the list of errands quickly. You might also tighten your physicality and increase the speed of your gestures. Combining the speed of speech and the rapidity of the physicality offers the impression that a great deal is happening quickly. It can activate the otherwise mundane list of events while underscoring the many things you had to accomplish on that hectic morning. Furthermore, speeding up and slowing down your speech and physicality is a good way to signal shifts in the perspective of the story. Imagine you're telling a story about being chased by a schoolyard bully as a child. You might narrate the chase quickly, breathlessly, and pumping your arms quickly to suggest the speed of your run. All of this would signal how you felt there-then, in the past, when the story took place. As you run from the bully, you fall and rip your pants—you pop out of the speed of narrating the chase to drop into a casual conversational tone to deliver the aside, "my mom was more worried about my pants than the bully," before jumping right back into the fast-paced delivery and arm-pumping movement of the chase. Through this example, you can see how shifting the pacing of the performance can help shift the point of view of the performance.

Just as important as speed are pause and stillness. Pause and stillness have the effect of drawing an audience's attention directly to you. People sometimes seem concerned that if they stop talking, the audience will stop listening, when, in fact, the opposite is true. A pause in the middle of a sentence can leave the audience metaphorically hanging on your words, waiting to hear what happens next. We can also think about pause as it relates to what is known as "timing." If you've ever seen someone tell a joke that fails, it may be because they did not "land" the punch line. The parts of the joke are all there, but they seem to fall in the wrong places. A dear colleague of mine pointed out to me that timing, is an embodied act. It is easy to think of it as serving a rhetorical function, part of the use of language, and it is that. But the breath, the space, pacing, and the eventual placing of a particular line right where you want it is something one does through the body. You may remember David's story from Chapter 4, which braided the challenges he faced getting along with his father with the conflict that arises in the Godzilla films. In one particularly affecting moment of the story, David broadly physicalizes and describes Godzilla fighting Mothra—having poisonous venom sprayed in his eyes and wailing in pain. At the peak of Godzilla's suffering, David abruptly drops all of the broad physicality, becomes still and silent, before looking at the audience and saying with just a hint of melancholy, "Middle school was hard." The sudden use of pause and stillness created a stunning contrast between his physical manifestation of Godzilla's titanic suffering and his inwardly focused preteen angst. The first time I saw David take this profound pause, it nearly knocked me out of my chair.

Final Thoughts on Embodiment

It can take time for some people to feel comfortable in their own bodies in front of other people. First, let me once again assure you that your body probably knows what to do, and if you listen to your body, it will lead you in the right direction. Most people naturally gesture in ways that emphasize what they are saying. Most people have an innate sense of timing, born from years of talking and hearing others speak. Most people naturally communicate emotion through their faces. As a storyteller, it is your job to listen to what your body naturally wants to do and then work to do what is most effective with intention. The process of listening to your body and intentionally shaping your embodiment requires rehearsal. You must be willing to begin by standing up in front of other people—hopefully people you trust—without a plan seeing what happens naturally. While you are up there, try to notice what your body wants to do, what choices you want to keep and accentuate, and what choices you want to discard. With each successive rehearsal, you can incorporate and sharpen the embodied practices you want to keep until your performance looks polished.

Questions to Consider

1 How do you think people see you when you stand in front of them? How can you make those perceptions work to your advantage?
2 Make a list of people who might appear in your story. What characteristics do they possess? How can you represent those characteristics simply and clearly through performance?
3 Select a portion of Mace's story below. How can you embody the content of that section in a way that matches the action of the story?

Housewarming
Created and Performed by Mace Gallagher

When I was young, I was obsessed with space exploration. My great-grandfather worked as a NASA photographer, and when I'd visit, we'd spend hours looking through his favorite shots. Then we'd grab some hot chocolate to keep our hands warm and head out to the backyard with his telescope already set up. I swear I could hear the moon and stars sing to me. I'd pick them apart through the telescope, searching for new planets, for asteroids, for *something* to call my own discovery.

Right now, however, I'm searching for other things. I'm standing in my closet, my happy place, my overflowing conglomeration of eclectic shit I'll probably only wear once. Also the place where I am currently engaged in a vicious staring match with the corduroy section… but it's not letting up any time soon. (With a huff), I shift my gaze to the sheers and decide on a red ruffled night robe. Looking at my selection, I reminisce on the countless weekend nights I've spent here, making red carpet get-ups and royal dinner outfits with no plans. But tonight, I *have* plans, I'm going *out*.

It's August of 2019, I've been invited to a housewarming party. But this isn't just any old housewarming, it's a *gay* housewarming. The host is an old friend of mine; we were close at the beginning of high school but had grown apart when he moved. This is our first time reuniting, and my first time meeting all of his new queer and trans friends. Plus, with a party theme like "bimbo theys and cowboy gays" I know I have to be dressed to the nines. So after a decent 200 hours or so of searching through everything I own, I complete my fit with red leather cowboy boots and a half-assed bedazzled face mask.

I hope to God that the mask is enough to hide the nerves evident on my face. At this point, I know that I *am* queer, but I've never really been in an all queer space before, and I didn't know how or if I even belonged there.

Upon arrival, I'm greeted by the only two people I recognize. Blake, the homeowner, and Chris, whom I haven't really seen or spoken to since middle school, but we had always been friendly. Apparently we were closer than I remember because immediately Chris took me on their arm and asked, "so… you're not straight, right?"

Of course they didn't really mean it like *that*, I don't think. You know, most gays are fine with straight people; they just don't want it… in front of them. I also knew that when someone as flamboyant as Chris said "straight" they meant cis AND straight.

So, I say no, because I'm not! I know that much. But then Chris gestures all grand and says, "oh, marvelous!!"(in a Carol Channing voice)

And, okay maybe it wasn't in that exact voice, but they did have a slight obsession with late career Carol Channing and had more than once told me they were planning on being "un-monogamous" that day.

But then Chris spun me like the dramatic old theatre soul they are and said, "so, who are you?"

Well, when I was 18, I really realized I was queer. Not for the first time, definitely. It's not hard to realize when growing up in a small southern town. Not when I'm in 7th grade and just trying to finish lunch, but that one group from science class is there, and they would never pass on an opportunity to remind me that I'm a dyke or faggot or whatever else they picked up from the internet. But it wasn't true. I wasn't either of those things, *really*.

In middle school, all I was insecure, lonely, and trying so hard not to let anyone know how I felt or who I associated with. The "who" being my mother, who is now married to a woman, and my best friend,

who knew he was trans at the age of 12. I became an excellent performer before I even joined theatre. I wore a costume not to play a
character, but to appease an audience that didn't really care about
appeasing me. Eventually, I wore my costume long enough to con-
vince everyone else that I was someone that I was not. And truthfully,
I didn't even know who or what I was because I've always had people
to decide that for me.

But here I am standing in the middle of a group of people I don't
know, listening to someone I haven't talked to in years half shout over
the karaoke to ask me who *I* was? I think about the mask on my face and
wonder if I would even be able to recognize myself without it. I wonder
how long it had been since I put it on. I didn't know. So I tell them, "I
don't know."

Now, I'm sure this all sounds very dramatic, but identity crises, especially those surrounded by queers in muscle suits and cowboy hats,
are usually very dramatic. Fortunately, while I was freaking out in my
fishnets, Chris seems totally unaffected. In fact, they are ecstatic.

(BEAT)

"Isn't that so exciting?" (Carol Channing voice)

They're *beaming* at me, and I had no idea *why* because *no* it was not
exciting; it was *terrifying* and I'm about to open my mouth to yell that,
but then I feel their hand on my arm.

The warmth that came with it travels beyond the point of contact, and
they looked at me and said,

"There's no rush, just do you, you'll find what you're looking for."

(BEAT)

I felt something then that I hadn't felt since I was seven years old,
in the backyard with my Gramps. Looking up at the sky on a clear
night, equipped with a star atlas and hot chocolate warming my tiny
fingers. He would tell me, "If you ever get stuck, I recommend head-
ing out there. With a little exploring, I'm sure you'll find what you're
looking for."

8 "My Hyper Fixation Was a Little More Sinister": Storytelling Persona and Your Relationship with the Audience

It all started simply as Dani expressed a familiar concern: she didn't have anything interesting to talk about. "Surely," I replied, "that can't be true." Before I could launch into my prepared speech about how everyone has something interesting to talk about, Dani replied, "Well, I guess I could talk about the time I thought this guy in my French class was on the FBI's Ten Most Wanted List." Fast forward to our showcase at the end of the semester, where the story finally came to fruition. Dani had a reoccurring device in the story where she would describe coincidental similarities that the guy in her French class shared with the criminal on the FBI's Most Wanted List. Each time one of the similarities came up, Dani would squint a little and say, "Suspicious." She also repeated the name of the criminal in question several times as the answer to questions like: "The guy in my French class rode a bike to school. You know who else rode a bike?" And she'd repeat the criminal's name. On the second night of our showcase, Dani was particularly "in the zone," as they say, and she nailed all these elements. The audience was feeling it too, and by the time she was halfway through the story, they were repeating "suspicious" and the name of the criminal right along with her. Dani noticed this happening and played it up. By the end of the story, she was like an orchestra conductor, waving her arms and signaling the audience, who would shout their responses in return. We had planned the use of repetition in the story to demonstrate the way this mystery stayed on her mind. We had not planned the audience response or Dani's in the moment response back to them. The whole experience was—I hesitate to say "magical"—but it was really something. Dani had created such a profound relationship with the audience that they became fully part of the performance.

There are two primary players in any storytelling situation: the storyteller and the audience. These two players are in a relationship together, and that relationship is complicated. The setting matters too, but, very often, you can't control where you're asked to perform. Regardless of whether you find that relationship taking place in a classroom, a coffee shop, someone's living room, or a theater, the fundamental elements of the relationship remain the same. In this chapter, we will first examine the storytelling persona that storytellers create. Second, we'll offer three different models for theorizing

DOI: 10.4324/9781003039266-8

the storyteller's relationship with the audience. Finally, we will bring your persona and the audience back together to see how these two can get along.

Crafting Your Performance Persona

Telling stories is no different from any other cultural practice. Storytellers have a set of narrative elements and performative strategies at their disposal that can be combined in any number of ways. After thousands of years of human beings telling stories, there is very little new under the sun when it comes to narrative elements and performance strategies. What makes stories interesting and special is the unique way those elements are combined and the way that combination is communicated. The way you combine all the elements of storytelling is what makes your performance special. Your intuitive take on the story, your unique embodiment of the story, and your particular voice in the story are the things no one across all of history can offer, even if there really is nothing new under the sun. All these elements—your perspective, your voice, your embodiment—combine to create your storytelling persona. This self that you produce is the self that the audience meets and interacts with in the performance. Most artists, and storytellers are no exception, start out by imitating the people who got them excited about making art. There is certainly nothing wrong with a faithful homage or even outright borrowing from others when it comes to style. But you can't flourish as an artist, until you first discover, accept, and learn to shape your authentic voice. Then you can place that authentic voice in conversation with an audience to create a performance event that accomplishes what you want to accomplish.

The phrase "authentic voice" is a puzzle in and of itself. To some readers, that phrase may imply a single voice, an unchanging voice, or a voice that has been waiting for you out there in the ethereal world of perfect forms, rather than something that is deliberately crafted. To others, the phrase "authentic voice" might evoke actual vocal training—the kind actors get to support their voice and help it carry across long distances. When I use the phrase "authentic voice" I don't mean any of those things. Your authentic voice might be best described this way: the sound and feeling of a performance that represents and validates your well-considered world view. That doesn't mean your voice is unchanging, and it doesn't mean it is not constructed. In fact, what you might imagine as your "authentic voice" is always changing and it is definitely constructed.

Who we are is always a work in progress. If you were to look back at a diary or journal you wrote in your early teenage years, you might find that version of yourself almost unrecognizable and maybe even comically cringe-worthy. But that teenage version of you passionately believed the things they were saying and feeling. Those feelings are no less valid just because you don't feel them anymore or because they were, perhaps, ill-informed. That was you, even if it is not you now. It is you in progress. Some people like to say that we are always both "being and becoming." That means that we are simultaneously being ourselves and becoming ourselves. The word philosophers use when discussing the state of being is *ontology*—or the study of the nature of being. When I think about the simultaneity of being and becoming, I like to think about fingernails. When you look down at your fingernails, there they are. You can't see it, but they are certainly growing, and the proof is that every now and then, you must trim or file them. Your identity is a little like those fingernails. People can see it and interact with it, but after a little time has passed, we can notice changes. This is important to remember when you're thinking about how you present yourself to others. If you are always changing, then the moment that the audience sees you is just a snapshot of who you are. If your identity is always in progress, then it is always a construction.

Sometimes this construction of persona is more obvious than others. Anyone who has worked in customer service, like a server in a restaurant, knows that they must put on a show—or adopt a persona—for the public as part of their job. Their "server persona" isn't a lie. It reflects who they really are but is also not entirely "true" in so far as it is not who they are all the time. It is constructed for a specific purpose, and we construct personas for ourselves for situations like that all the time. This is yet another way in which our identities are always in motion. The feeling that someday our identity will be fully settled, that we will finally grow up or just be ourselves, is a comforting fiction that people like to tell themselves and each other. Even though this is the case, and perhaps because this is the case, we can't always see ourselves constructing our identity. Storytellers don't have the luxury of being oblivious to how they are perceived. The question for storytellers is: what feels real and right, right now? The answer to that question is presented through a constructed self that further communicates your authentic voice.

The expression of your authentic voice as a storyteller is expressed through your performance persona. For most storytellers, the performance persona is an amplified version of who you are in your regular life, staged for performance. It is not a character that does not resemble your everyday self. You've probably heard someone describe an actor as "disappearing into his character," and on some level that's an actor's job: to become someone else in front of people. Storytellers, on the other hand, are trying to make their authentic self-appear before an audience. Writing about personal essays (a close cousin to personal narrative storytelling), Carl H. Klaus contends, "… the 'person' in the personal essay is a written construct, a fabricated thing, a character of sorts—the sound of its voice a by-product of carefully chosen words, its recollection of experience … much tidier than the mess of: memories, thoughts, and feelings arising in one's consciousness" (1). Personal storytelling also presents a deliberately constructed performance persona. This performance is just another role we play among many: sibling, child, romantic partner, student, friend, and so forth. Your performance self is a side of you, a representation of you, a version of you. Many books have been and will be written on the subject of identity formation, but this is not one of them. For our purposes, we need only accept the following: we use narrative elements and performative strategies to construct a performance persona, and that persona is the part of our self that encounters the audience. The fact that your performance self is carefully constructed means that you can work on crafting it into what you want it to be. You're not just stuck with one immutable self. However, you should remember that you are telling true stories about yourself. The performance persona you create for yourself needs to be an honest one. So, how do you do that?

One way to make sense of the self we present in front of others is as a collection of signifiers that are always situated in culture. Your height, hair, gender presentation, clothes, posture, gestures, tone of voice, facial expressions, and so forth all tell an audience something about you. We don't always like the idea of an audience making assumptions about someone based on their appearance, but audiences tend to do it anyway, so it's worth considering before you stand on stage. Furthermore, what you say and how you say it will also lead an audience to interpret your performance persona in particular ways. If you use profanity and make jokes at the expense of others, or if you use self-deprecating humor and show care for others, either way, it will tell the audience something about you. Which is not to say you need to change yourself to meet the expectations of the audience. After all, you being you is what makes your stories special. However, storytellers do need to think critically about how they are perceived and work to anticipate how an audience will feel when they hear and see them.

Another way to think of the construction of your performance persona in personal narrative storytelling is to try and communicate a slightly exaggerated version of who you usually are when people meet you. Performance for a live audience requires that you amplify who you are so that it reaches the entire room. And, as a general rule, the more people you are trying to reach with a message, the less complicated the message can be. So, if what you are trying to communicate is who you are, you need to exaggerate, and thus simplify, who you are just a bit. Once again, this exaggeration of the self requires you to think through how people see you.

The careful application of self-reflection can help you see yourself as the audience sees you and then control how you are perceived. If there is something about your self-presentation or comportment that you think might get in the way of your relationship with the audience, usually the best choice is to just say the quiet part out loud and own it. Kit, whom you met elsewhere in this book, crystallized this perspective. Remember how Kit began their story in the previous chapter? One morning, Kit came to class and got up to workshop that story. Kit was dressed the way they usually were in those days: big boots, a ripped denim vest, piercings, and a green mohawk. Kit looked at us with a straight faced and said, "You probably can't tell by looking at me now, but I was a pretty weird kid." The room burst out in laughter, and from then on, Kit controlled how people saw them. The lesson was clear: lean into who you are, and, more often than not, the audience will like you for doing so.

Now, some readers out there may not feel particularly good about themselves and how they are perceived by others. When you imagine yourself on stage in front of an audience, you may not like what you see. Or you may not think the audience will like what they see. In other words, there may be readers who don't think their authentic voice and performance persona are particularly efficacious in performance. Often, these concerns are rooted in how you feel about yourself, not in the way an audience perceives you. Audiences, in general, want you to succeed. I want to assure you: whoever you are, you are perfectly suitable to become a storyteller. Your individual take on the world, the reality of your material body, and the sound of your voice are all acceptable. With a little effort, you can craft all that you are into the storyteller you want to be.

The next step in the process is to think about the people you'll be meeting in the performance: the audience. In what follows, I offer a few different perspectives on theorizing audiences. No one perspective is superior to the others, and you can integrate them in ways that make sense to you. I have also, admittedly, simplified these concepts for the purposes of this book. These theories simply offer a set of frameworks through which you can begin understanding those people you'll be encountering in performance.

Theorizing the Audience

The audience makes up the other side of that equation. The word "audience" has Latin and French origins and originally meant, "to hear." Since then, the term has come to refer to any group that congregates (in shared physical space, like a theatre audience or in virtual space, like a television audience) to witness and interact with what could be broadly referred to as cultural content. Television shows, books, speeches, print advertisements, and even street signs (if you're inclined to extend the metaphor) are just a few examples of cultural content that has an intended audience. On the surface, the typical audience for a performance may seem like a simple thing: a group of people gathered to witness and enjoy a performance. The word "audience" can be a noun, referring to a group of people witnessing a performance, or it can be a verb, referring to the *act* of witnessing a performance. A group of individuals come together and witness, encounter, engage with, and co-create performance. Sometimes they literally get involved, like in Dani's story at the top of this chapter. Together, the audience members create a kind of living, interactive, composite whole. How this happens is one of the most pervasive mysteries of performance theory. In what follows, we'll look at both metaphors and theories that help us understand how audiences and what they do.

But first, it is worth noting that the performance self, as described above, and the audience, as described above, and the relationship between the two are all elusive and ephemeral. They don't sit still, and they are prone to slipping out of your hands when you try to hold them in one place. It is no wonder, then, that storytelling itself is an elusive and ephemeral art. It conjures up images and emotions that we see and feel in profound ways, but when the performance is over those potent feelings seem to whisp away like smoke or a dream. The following three theoretical frameworks that follow help us get a hold of that elusive and ephemeral relationship.

Psychoanalysis and the Third

The first model for thinking about the relationship between the storyteller and the audience wasn't actually intended to be used to explain that relationship at all. Karl Jung, one of the foundational figures in psychoanalysis, posited the concept called The Third. In psychoanalysis, this concept refers to the symbolic coming together of a patient and an analyst to create a third thing, their relationship. This union of the two transcends the component parts and has its own potential for meaning-making. It takes you and me interacting together— even if that interaction is, at times, imagined—to create meaning. That interaction creates something that transcends both individuals. This phenomenon reminds me of two celebrities who start dating and are given a couple name that combines parts of their names, thus creating a third entity that joins the two and transcends them both. The transcendent function of The Third, "is an attempt to describe the psychic function that is involved in the creation of *meaning*—it is an account of the meaning-making function of the psyche that suggests meaning to be the outcome of a process of opposition between two or more opposing elements that are somehow transcended in the creation of a third with a new level of complexity" (Coleman 566). In other words, we don't make meaning alone, we need other forces and figures to push it off for meaning-making to occur. Coleman goes on to explain that "The emergence of the third could also be described as the development of a capacity for symbolic imagination or simply *imaginal capacity*" or "the capacity to formulate and creatively explore images of one's own psychic life and the world in a way that feels fully real yet distinct from the actuality of the external world" (566). The exploration of "one's own psychic life and the world in a way that feels fully real yet distinct from the actuality of the external world" could be another accurate definition of the purpose of personal narrative storytelling.

In storytelling, The Third is created in the transcendent relationship between the audience and performer. At its best, storytelling creates a union between the audience and the performer that allows them to be on the "same page," so to speak. The audience is seeing and feeling what the storyteller is seeing and feeling. What's more, the audience is sharing this experience with the storyteller *and* with each other. It is a transcendent experience that allows for what Coleman calls the "imaginal capacity" or the capacity to imagine psychic symbols. In this case, those psychic symbols are the ephemeral images called up by the storyteller and meaningfully imagined by the audience. When a performer describes a performance using the idiom, "I had the audience in the palm of my hand," they may be trying to put words to the shared symbolic experience between audience and performer.

The creation of The Third is only really possible when the performer and a critical mass of audience members understand each other. That means that homogenous audiences—audiences that share characteristics with the performer and with one another—may have an easier time having a shared experience. Each year in the United States, the little town of Jonesborough, Tennessee, hosts the National Storytelling Festival. The Festival is like the World Series of professional storytelling, drawing storytellers from across the country and from overseas. The streets in the town are cordoned off, enormous circus-sized tents are erected, and for three days, thousands of people come from far and wide to see individuals stand on stage and tell stories of all kinds. The festival grew out of the American storytelling revival of the 1970s, which itself was inspired largely by Appalachian folk traditions. As a result, many of the most popular storytellers have a conspicuously Southern bent to them. The audience is mostly older, mostly white, and clearly financially secure enough to spend money on tickets and travel to attend the festival. The first time I attended the festival, I brought a relatively diverse group of traditionally aged college students with me. I was shocked to discover that they were almost the only people in their teens and 20s attending the festival, and some of the only people of color. The largely homogenous audience seemed, at times, to be having an entirely different audience experience than we were. That's understandable because the event was tailored to fit that homogenous audience. Together, they were able to imagine the idyllic Southern upbringing so often evoked in the stories Southern storytellers tell. Hundreds of people laughed together at jokes and grew quiet together in dramatic moments as they had a shared capacity for imagining the story they heard.

The festival organizers seem aware that their audience is aging and that the history and structure of the festival may make some potential audience members feel unwelcome. When most people attend an event, I think they like to look around and see other people who look like them. What's more, idealized stories about the South, which has a long and troubled history (to say the least), can easily exclude difficult realities—especially about race—that need to be addressed. But it is not my intention here to begin a critique of The National Storytelling Festival. For our purposes, the festival represents a sort of closed system where a huge group of people have shared experience that creates this other, this Third. That all being said, most if not all, audiences have a shared set of human emotions such as: love, fear, shame, hope, desire, anxiety, disappointment, and joy. Tapping into these emotions can help storytellers and audiences join up to create the sort of Third entity that makes meaning.

Audience Reception Theory

Media theorist Stuart Hall was born and raised in Jamaica, back when Jamaica was still a British colony. He eventually traveled to England to study, and throughout his life as a colonial subject and as a Black person living in a predominantly white country, Hall was acutely aware of the ways messages are presented to create meaning. Specifically, Hall was interested in the ways messages reinforced hegemony, another word for power and influence. It is surely no surprise to you that the people who create cultural content have the hegemonic power to influence the perception of their audience. However, when Hall began thinking about media and its influence, most scholarship and criticism assumed that all meaning resided with the author and the audiences were, essentially, passive receptacles for that meaning. Hall picked up the reception theory of German literary critic Hans-Robert Juass and ran with those ideas. Hall's work on audience reception theory was originally applied to traditional media, like television and movies, but it is equally applicable to the relationship between a live audience and a storyteller.

In short, Hall argues that the creators of cultural content, for example, television shows, encode the content with messages and meanings. Those messages and meanings may be intentional, to communicate a particular story or set of values the creators want to share. Those messages and meanings may also be unintentional, communicating something that wasn't intended but seems to be present nonetheless. Those messages and meanings are also related to the surrounding culture, other stories, the expectations of the medium, and so on. When an audience decodes the message as the creators intended, this is known as the dominant reading. When the audience inflects the dominant reading with their own perspective, this is known as a negotiated reading. When the audience sees the dominant reading as existing in direct conflict with their perception of the world, this is known as an oppositional reading. So, for example, if you watch a television show and come away from it having interpreted it just as the creators intended, you've engaged in the dominant reading of the show. If you finish the show having made your own sense of the show's intended message, you've engaged in a negotiated reading of the show. If you walk away from that show rejecting its message and understanding it as problematic for someone like you, you've engaged in an oppositional reading. These three categories are a useful framework for you as someone who is making stories because they represent a spectrum of audience responses that might occur when people engage with your work. In most situations, as a storyteller, you want the audience to take up the dominant or negotiated reading of your story so that they understand the point of view you're trying to communicate. If, on the other hand, your audience takes up an oppositional reading of your story, it is likely that your intended message has been lost on them. This is, admittedly, a simplified version of Hall's thinking. Helen Davis' *Understanding Stuart Hall* offers a more comprehensive look at his work. In this case, we're using reception theory as a heuristic way of thinking about how the relationship between producer and audience.

At this point, we need to draw a significant distinction between the mass media that Hall studied, and the more localized content that most personal narrative storytellers create. Hall supposes that the messages produced in mass media, like film and television, will always necessarily reproduce the interests of people in power. This is, in part, because producing mass media requires significant resources, and the people who control those resources aren't likely to produce content that works against their interests. What's more, producing media for a mass audience, which these days means a global audience, requires media creators to appeal to big, dominant narratives that make sense to the largest number of people. Those big messages often leave a lot of people out, erasing identities that don't fit neatly within the dominant narrative. This is a function of hegemony (or power), and it is one of the ways that oppression is perpetuated. Those messages are, almost by definition, dominant narratives.

Alternatively, the creation and distribution of personal storytelling does not require significant financial or material resources. At most, it only requires the storyteller to have a pen and a notebook, and you can probably get away with not even having that. Furthermore, personal narrative storytelling is almost always created for a specific, localized audience—not a large, global audience. For the most part, the more people who need to understand a message, the less complex the message can be. The inverse is also true, a message meant for a small, specific audience can be far more sophisticated because it needs to be interpreted by relatively few people. This all means that personal storytelling is well positioned to act as an intervention and disruption into oppressive dominant narratives. The potential for intervention and disruption means that storytellers have a significant obligation to think about the good a story can do, undermining oppressive practices. This is a crucial departure from Hall's theories of audience reception based on the shift from mass media to a localized medium like storytelling.

Jacob spent a short amount of time working at a local grocery store. I say a short amount of time because he quit after a few months because he grew weary of the "family" ethos that the store tried to encourage in its employees. If the employees were a family, Jacob reasoned, the store could easily have more of them than was appropriate and fail to pay a fair wage. After all, family must stick together. Jacob crafted a very funny story about his days working at the grocery store, using humor to skewer the ingenuine strategies of capitalist organizations, like grocery stores, use to manipulate their employees. As he pointed out, "You know who else calls themselves a family? The Manson Family and the Mafia." Jacob guessed that most audience members had not thought too much about this part of the grocery store experience, so he offered an oppositional message that challenged the power structures they'd grown used to.

Jacob's example is a relatively light critique of capitalist systems. If your identity has historically been marginalized and if you are a person who has experienced oppression—perhaps by precisely the sort of people watching your story—then crafting a message that offers an oppositional reading in your story can reassert your power.

A Phenomenological Approach to Audiences

The word "phenomenology" can sound a little funny and a little intimidating. When you discover that it is a philosophical discipline engineered by brilliant German and French philosophers, it can sound even more daunting to understand. However, despite its impressive sounding name, phenomenology is not so complicated and is a useful tool for understanding the relationship between storyteller and audience. As you probably already know, the suffix "ology" means "the study of" and is often attached to words to denote an intellectual discipline—such as psychology or sociology. The first part of the word "phenomen" means, strictly speaking, "a thing appearing into view," or in other words, something that we encounter. When we encounter things, phenomenologists suppose that we direct our intention at that thing and our encounter with the thing. So, phenomenology is the study of what happens when we encounter things. That may sound a bit vague, but imagine asking questions like: how do we take up and make sense of what we witness? How do apprehend something with our senses? How do we experience, in this case, a performance with our sensing and experiencing body?

For storytellers, phenomenology is a useful tool for imagining their way into the experience of the audience. If, as we said at the start of this book, storytelling is the art of getting a group of people to see, think, and feel the same thing at the same time, then understanding how and where audiences point their intentions can be exceptionally useful to a storyteller. In order to do this, one must adopt a phenomenological attitude. Robert Sokolowski describes the distinction between the phenomenological attitude and the natural attitude this way: the natural attitude can be described as our "default perspective, the one we start from, the one we are in originally," while the phenomenological attitude, "is the focus we have when we reflect upon the natural attitude and all the internationalities that occur within it" (42). In other words, the storyteller can adopt a phenomenological attitude to critically consider what the subjective encounter with a story will feel like for an audience. The adoption of this phenomenological attitude also implies a self-consciousness on the part of the storyteller, an awareness of oneself in relation to the audience.

You may recall Ben's story from Chapter 4. Ben felt sure about his decision to tell the story of a dear friend who took his own life at a young age. The story was meant to be a tribute to his friend and an inspirational tale for anyone who felt hopeless. Ben and his friend both participated in Boy Scouts, and this young person's death shocked the whole troupe. Ben began his story by telling a funny anecdote about camping with his friend and the other Scouts. When the anecdote reached its comedic peak, Ben abruptly revealed that his friend killed himself a short time later. The effect was jarring to listeners, but Ben wanted to give the audience a taste of the shock he and his friends felt when they heard the news. That desire and that strategy, it seemed to us, were valid and compelling. We tried to guess how an audience might respond. Eventually, Ben ran his story in front of a test audience to see how this abrupt left turn into tragedy would play outside of our coaching sessions. The test audience was uncomfortable with the abruptness of the reveal. Not only was it upsetting, but it seemed to them as if Ben wasn't sufficiently careful with his friend's memory. Ultimately, the test audience suggested simply slowing the reveal down so that it didn't happen so quickly. Before the reveal, Ben would pause, his body language would change, and his facial expression would change—all to signal that things were about to get serious. The test audience pushed Ben to adopt a phenomenological attitude and a critical perspective and carefully consider the felt experience of the audience. Ben spent a good deal of time critically considering his relationship. He did so by stepping outside what simply felt right in his natural attitude and stepping into a phenomenological attitude.

The truth is, there is no substitute for experience when it comes to creating a relationship with an audience. The more you get up in front of people, the more comfortable you'll feel doing it. However, in the meantime, understanding your performance persona and theorizing how you can relate to audiences are important steps toward creating a successful relationship with an audience.

Questions to Consider

1 Write down a list of all the demographic characteristics of the audience you plan to perform for, as far as you can tell. What about your story is relatable to them, and what about your story might be unfamiliar? How are you similar, and how do you differ from your expected audience?
2 Ask a trusted friend to describe you. What are your most notable characteristics? What do you commonly say? What is your general attitude toward life? Have your trusted friend help you make a list of the qualities they see in you.
3 Write a few paragraphs describing how you want the audience to see you while you are performing. What about you makes creating that perception achievable, and what might stand in your way?

"Dani's Most Wanted"
Created and Performed by Dani Ramos

I'm normally a very well-prepared student, but this day on my schedule in my French 1101 class, I wasn't prepared. I was never prepared for this day. I had left all of my writing utensils at home, and I had to do that thing that college students do where you turn to your neighbor, who you haven't spoken to all semester, and ask for a pencil.
   [Turns around]
   "Hey, do you mind if I borrow a pencil? Thanks."
   [Looks intensely, opens mouth wide]

I didn't know what it was at that moment. I couldn't put my finger on it, but there was something about this guy that was sitting behind me—his mischievous glint in his piercing blue eyes, the crooked smile that he gave me, and the barbaric way that he just dug into his black duffle bag for a pencil. I don't know what it was, but it was something. [*Grabs imaginary pencil*] Thanks.

[*Quickly turns back around as if to double take*]

Sacre bleu!

or as English speakers would say, holy shit. I had never seen this man before in my entire life, but I remember seeing his face from the ages of nine to 12 on TV on a monthly basis. How, you ask?

Well, here's the thing: as kids, each of us kind of had our own hyperfixations. Me, personally, as a six-year-old, my hyperfixation was a little more sinister. See, after a long day of first grade and swimming lessons and general childhood antics, I like to curl up on the couch with a tall glass of apple juice on the rocks, had a plate of macaroni and cheese and chicken fingers, and I liked to watch my favorite show of all time, [*Deepens voice uses imaginary microphone*] America's Most Wanted hosted by John Walsh. I don't know what it was about this show, and I was a fairly curious kid as a child, of course, and for some reason, this show really just scratched an itch in my underdeveloped six-year-old brain. And it taught me so many things about these criminals, what they did, their aliases, and where they could possibly be hiding. And it taught me enough to give a side eye to anyone that I walked past a little too closely in the grocery store.

And I guess these habits just kind of followed me into my adult life because I was convinced that this man that was sitting right behind me in French class was none other than Jason Derek Brown. Who's Jason Derek Brown, you may ask? I'll give you the rundown. [*Deepens voice*] November 4, 2004, it was a hot, sunny dry day in Phoenix, Arizona, and Jason Derek Brown shot and killed a police officer that was guarding an armored truck and made away with $56,000 in cash in a black double bag on a bicycle. Now you'd think that they could cash him fairly easily because he got away on a bicycle, but the thing about Jason Derek Brown, is that his visage was just so bland, so generic, so Wonder Bread, middle-aged white guy that he just blended into a crowd. He just disappeared and hid in plain sight.

And I don't know, I just made with that information what I could, and this guy fit the bill. I just went ahead and I thought that this guy was my perp. I was on this case, and I was on it hard. I made way with all the evidence that I could after looking at the FBI's most wanted list for like the fifth time that week, and I had to make a list of all of the evidence that I could to match up with Jason Derek Brown with my classmate. One of Jason Derek Brown's aliases was simply Derek Brown. My classmate's name was Daniel, if that really was his name, and those start with a D. [*Touches chin*] Suspicious. Jason Derek Brown spoke French and English fluently. Daniel is in a French class. [*Touches chin*] Suspicious. Jason Derek Brown made his great escape on a bicycle. Daniel rode to school on a bicycle every single day. [*Rubs chin*] Suspicious.

I took this information and did whatever I could to watch Daniel in any way. Now, in a perfect world, I would have all the toys the FBI had—all these hidden mics, and these bulletproof vests, and a SWAT team. But this wasn't a perfect world, and all I really had to my name was a zebra print taser and my charming personality. But what I lacked in equipment, I made up for and stealth. I made it a point to make sure that Daniel never left my sight. So what I did is I made a habit to get to class a good five minutes before Daniel did, and I would make small talk with him, talk it up a little bit before I had to do some French, and then I would let Daniel walk away before I did. And I'd wait 30 seconds before I ran right into his general vicinity, and I made sure to leave and follow him at a three cars pace.

Now, I made sure that it was a three cars pace because if it was any closer, he'd be on to me. If it was any further away, he'd blend into the crowd, and I wouldn't be able to tell him from any other white guy on campus. I made sure that he was in the cafeteria, I was in the cafeteria. If he was in the library, I made sure that I was four tables away, reading the same book that he was. Whatever he was reading, I was reading. [*Bounces excitedly*] Whatever he was talking to, I was talking to. Whatever he was eating, I was eating. So the semester went on and I finally had a golden opportunity to catch this guy. It was our final, and our final was for French class is that we had to meet up with a group of four and make a conversation in French between a group of friends. I took this opportunity to say, [*turns around to reenact*] "Hey Daniel, you want to be in a group together?"

So I made sure that Daniel and I were in a group together, but the only conversation that I was wanting to have with Daniel is getting him to commit and confess to the crimes that he did. [*points finger*] So luckily, on the day that we were trying to meet up for a little lunch date to discuss our project, we managed to sit in the cafeteria, but our other two classmates were running late. So for the first couple of minutes of our lunch date, it was just me and Daniel.

"So, Daniel, do you have family in the area?"

"No, not really. Most of them are on the West Coast."

"Oh, okay. You have family on the West Coast?"

"Yeah. I'm probably going to go visit them maybe later on in a break, like I'm turning 31 and my birthday's coming up so I'm going to go see them on my birthday."

"Oh, okay. So your birthday's coming up. Cool. When's your birthday?"

"It's the day after Christmas."

"Oh, [*high pitched*] so you're a Capricorn."

"Yeah. I mean, I don't really know much about that stuff, but I guess. Yeah."

"Oh, *[higher pitched]* well, I'm a Libra. Could you excuse me for just a second?"

Oh my God. How did I not ask for his birthday? That's probably like of the most important pieces of information that I could've asked for. After I ran off from the table, I made sure to look up the Wikipedia article, Jason Derek Brown, for the 20th time that week just to verify the information. *[Holds imaginary notebook]* Finally, it was all coming together now. All the information was coming together! What did Jason Derek Brown make his great escape on? *[Points]* A bicycle. What did Daniel ride to school on every day? *[Gestures to crowd to answer]*

A bicycle.

What did Jason Derek Brown have on his back the day of November 4th, 2004? A black double bag. What did Daniel come to school with every day? *[Gets crowd to answer:]*

A black duffle bag!

Now, Daniel just said his Zodiac sign. It was a Capricorn. What was Jason Brown's zodiac sign?

He was a Cancer! *[With hands in the air drops head in disappointment]* He was a Cancer of all things. Oh my god. *[Puts hands on head]* When I looked at the Wikipedia article, it said that his birthday is July 1st, 1969. A Cancer?! God, not only was his birthday completely off, he was a whole 20 years older than Daniel.

The case was cracked, not cracked, it was cold at this point. I had no evidence to pin against Daniel. Maybe he literally was just a random guy that sat behind me in French class. Maybe his name really was Daniel. Maybe he probably thought that I was just some random girl who had an obsessive crush on him. The semester went by without a hitch, and from what I last remembered, our French class said that we were going to register for French two together since we all really liked each other, and I went ahead and did that. I registered for French two in the spring, but as I did that, I went ahead and looked through the roster just to make sure that everyone was in our class.

But as I was looking through the class roster, there was a name missing. Daniel wasn't registered for the class. Okay, it's not weird at all. I went ahead and dropped that unit of the class and registered for the other one. You know, just to check if Daniel was in it. I registered, looked at the class roster, and looked for Daniel. Daniel, *[Scrolling through list]* Daniel, Daniel, Daniel…. No Daniel. Okay, still not weird, so I went ahead and I checked the group chat that we made for class. *[Pulls out imaginary phone]* I scrolled through, went ahead, and checked. Daniel was one of the first people to leave the group chat. I don't know. That was a little weird to me. To me personally, I just find it a little strange that Jason Derek Brown and Daniel are both at large. Suspicious.

References

Althusser, Louis. "Ideology." *Performance Analysis*, Ed. Colin Counsell and Laurie Wolf, Routledge, 2001, pp. 32–43.

Bauman, Richard. *Verbal Art as Performance*. Newbury House Publishers, 1977.

Bell, Elizabeth. "Toward a Pleasure-Centered Economy: Wondering a Feminist Aesthetics of Performance." *Text & Performance Quarterly*, vol. 15, 1995, pp. 99–121.

Ben Driss, Hager. "Nomadic Genres: The Case of the Short Story Cycle." *Mosaic: An Interdisciplinary Critical Journal*, vol. 51, no. 2, 2018, pp. 59–74.

Bowles, Meg, et al. *How to Tell a Story: The Essential Guide to Memorable Storytelling from The Moth*. Crown, 2022.

Burke, Kenneth. *Language as Symbolic Action*. University of California Press, 1966.

Campbell, Joseph. *The Hero with a Thousand Faces*. New World Library, 2008.

Colman, Warren. "Symbolic Conceptions: The Idea of the Third". *Journal of Analytical Psychology*, vol. 52, 2007, pp. 565–583

Corey, Fredrick. "The Personal: Against the Master Narrative." *The Future of Performance Studies: Visions and Revisions*. Ed. Sheron J. Dailey. National Communication Association,1998, pp. 249–53.

Davis, Helen. *Understanding Stuart Hall*. E-Book, Sage, 2004.

Gillett, William. *The Illusion of the First Time*. Franklin Classics, 2018.

Gingrich-Philbrook, Craig. "Just a Bunch of Therapy: Challenging the Dismissive." *Text & Performance Quarterly*, vol. 37, no. 2, 2017, pp. 138–144.

Grothe, Mary. *Never Let a Fool Kiss You or a Kiss Fool You*. Penguin Books, 2002.

Klaus, Carl. *The Made-Up Self: Impersonation in the Personal Essay*. University of Iowa Press, 2010.

Leitman, Margo. *Long Story Short: The Only Storytelling Guide You'll Ever Need*. Sasquatch Books, 2015.

Luppa, Nick, Borst, Terry. *Stories and Simulations for Serious Games*. Routledge, 2006.

Lyotard, Jean-François. *The Postmodern Condition: A Report on Knowledge*. Manchester University Press, 1984.

Park-Fuller, Linda. "Performing Absence: The Staged Personal Narrative as Testimony." *Text and Performance Quarterly*, vol. 20, no. 1, 2000, pp. 20–42.

Peters, John Durham. *Speaking into the Air a History of the Idea of Communication*. University of Chicago Press, 1999.

Scott, Julie-Ann. "The Visceral Remains: Revealing the Human Desire for Performance Through Personal Narratives of Alzheimer's Disease." *Text & Performance Quarterly*, vol. 39, no. 2, 2019, pp. 116–134.

Sokolowski, Robert. *Introduction to Phenomenology.* Cambridge University Press, 2003.
Stephenson Shaffer, Tracy. "Performance Tells It Slant." *Text & Performance Quarterly*, vol. 36, no. 1, 2016, pp. 1–5.
Turner, Victor. *The Anthropology of Performance.* PAJ Publications, 1988.
Vonnegut, Kurt. "The Shapes of Stories." *Openculture.com*, https://www.openculture.com/2014/02/kurt-vonnegut-masters-thesis-rejected-by-u-chicago.html, accessed 29 Oct. 2022.

Index